THE LEOPARD

Look for these and other books in the
Lucent Endangered Animals and Habitats series:

The Amazon Rain Forest
The Bald Eagle
Bats
The Bear
Birds of Prey
The Cheetah
Chimpanzees
The Condor
Coral Reefs
The Cougar
The Crocodile
Dolphins and Porpoises
The Elephant
The Galápagos Islands
The Giant Panda

The Gorilla
The Jaguar
The Koala
The Manatee
The Oceans
The Orangutan
Owls
The Rhinoceros
Seals and Sea Lions
The Shark
Snakes
The Tiger
Turtles and Tortoises
The Whale
The Wolf

Other related titles in the Lucent Overview series:

Acid Rain
Endangered Species
Energy Alternatives
Garbage
The Greenhouse Effect
Hazardous Waste
Ocean Pollution
Oil Spills
Ozone
Pesticides
Population
Rain Forests
Recycling
Saving the American Wilderness
Vanishing Wetlands
Zoos

THE LEOPARD

BY KAREN POVEY

Endangered
Animals &
Habitats

LUCENT
BOOKS ®

THOMSON
GALE

San Diego • Detroit • New York • San Francisco • Cleveland • New Haven, Conn. • Waterville, Maine • London • Munich

LIBRARY OF CONGRESS CATALOGING-IN-PUBLICATION DATA

Povey, Karen D., 1962–
    The leopard / by Karen Povey.
    v. cm. — (Endangered animals & habitats)
    Includes bibliographical references and index (p.).
    Summary: Discusses the various subspecies of leopard, reasons for their endangered
status, their conflicts with human beings, and efforts to conserve the leopard.
    Contents: Meet the leopards—Habitat loss—Conflicts between leopards and people—
Leopard research and conservation—The future of leopards.
      ISBN 1-56006-921-X (hardback : alk. paper)
    1. Leopard—Juvenile literature. 2. Endangered species—Juvenile literature.
[1. Leopard. 2. Endangered species.] I. Title. II. Series.
      QL737.C23 P69 2003
      599.75′54—dc21

                                              2002003588

Printed in the United States of America

Contents

Introduction

SINCE THE DAWN of history, people have regarded wild cats with fascination and awe. Their mysterious nature has inspired many myths and legends, their grace and beauty have influenced art, and their strength and power have caused warriors and kings to adopt their images as symbols of might. Early civilizations revered cats of all kinds; the ancient Egyptians, for example, considered them the embodiments of gods. Leopards were one of many species of wild cat to receive this exalted status. African kings considered the leopard, with its courage and cunning, to be a worthy symbol of their reign. Statues and paintings recovered in many prehistoric sites associate leopards with fertility goddesses, and legends of supernatural leopards are known to many cultures.

Although many people today attribute the same qualities to wild cats that inspired the ancients, cats in recent times have suffered dramatically as a result of the rapidly increasing human population. In fact, wild cats are among the most threatened of the world's mammals. The International Union for the Conservation of Nature (IUCN), a conservation organization that tracks the status of rare wildlife globally, lists seventeen species and twenty-three subspecies of wild cats on its 2000 IUCN Red List of Threatened Species.

The IUCN Red List includes all three leopard species—leopard, snow leopard, and clouded leopard. They are suffering from declining numbers as a result of deforestation and other destructive human activities taking place in their

All three species of leopard are among the world's endangered wild cats.

natural habitats. Most serious of all is the growing threat of illegal hunting, or poaching, which threatens to wipe out leopard populations in some areas. For some leopards, the situation is critical. One type of leopard, the Amur leopard, living in the forests of the Russian Far East, is dangerously close to extinction; only thirty to forty individuals remain in the wild.

The status of other leopards, however, has proven difficult to determine. Leopards are secretive, elusive animals and as a consequence are challenging to study in the wild. Estimating the population of some species, such as the rarely glimpsed clouded leopard, is nearly impossible. Researchers currently in the field are attempting to collect information on the biology and behavior of these animals that they hope will help them develop effective conservation strategies.

One important consideration for leopard conservation is encouraging the participation of people who live near leopards and are affected by their activities. By helping people solve problems associated with leopards that kill their livestock or threaten their families' safety, conservationists are discovering that they can encourage communities to develop new attitudes about protecting the cats.

Conservation efforts

Working cooperatively with local people in safeguarding leopards will likely be the key to these cats' survival. Participation in conservation efforts by governments, private organizations, and zoos has already yielded some promising results. For example, the snow leopard and the people who share its home in the Himalayan Mountains have already benefited from this type of partnership. In exchange for protecting snow leopards and adopting ways of managing their livestock to enhance coexistence with the big cats, the local people have been provided with opportunities to increase their standard of living and earn desperately needed money.

In addition to conservation programs in countries that are home to wild leopard populations, captive breeding programs in zoos around the world are dedicated to preserving leopards. Despite the efforts under way to preserve leopards and their habitats, the possibility exists that wild leopards may someday become extinct, with only remnant populations living in zoos. So by scientifically managing breeding populations in zoos, biologists hope to maintain the bloodlines of rare leopards as a sort of insurance against their possible disappearance in the wild.

Conservationists remain optimistic that the extinction of wild leopards can be prevented. However, the challenges they face are great. If ways can be found to reduce conflicts between leopards and people, protect leopard habitat, and enforce laws against illegal hunting, leopards might have a chance at a secure future.

Conservationists often work with local governments and zoos to protect leopard populations from extinction.

1

Meet the Leopards

WILD CATS ARE among the most recognizable of all the world's animals. From early childhood, most people can easily distinguish tigers, lions, and leopards from one another. Beyond their obvious similarities and differences, however, wild cats and their relationship within the animal kingdom are not well understood by most people. To understand the wild cat family, it is helpful to look at their place in the animal classification system used by scientists.

Cat classification

The animal classification system groups animals according to shared characteristics. These groupings are determined by the animals' physical similarities, such as features of the skull, teeth, and skeleton, and by the development of their young. Sometimes patterns of behavior, such as feeding and courtship, are also considered. Increasingly, scientists are applying a new tool to the task of classification: the analysis of the genetic makeup of the species. Laboratory analysis of an animal's DNA can help scientists determine what other species are its closest genetic cousins. This new procedure has allowed biologists to classify animals with much more accuracy than they were able to in the past. In many cases, this information has resulted in changes in the existing classification system as previously unrecognized relationships between species have been revealed.

Within this classification system, all cats, both wild and domestic, belong to the Felidae family. This family is divided into two subfamilies, the Pantherinae and the Felinae. The Pantherinae includes all the species of leopards, as well as other "big cats"—lions, tigers, and jaguars. The Felinae contains the "small cats" such as the serval, ocelot, and common housecat. The distinctions of "small" and "big" cat can be misleading, however. For example, some small cats, such as the mountain lion, are much larger than some big cats, such as the clouded leopard. But those titles are popular, not scientific, distinctions.

Members of the Pantherinae subfamily are further classified into twelve distinct species. Each species has a unique scientific name, in Latin, consisting of a genus and species. The genus, or first part of the scientific name, is sometimes shared by several species, indicating that they are more closely related to each other than to other cats in the same subfamily.

 ## Cat Design: Driven by Meat Eating
In her book *The Tribe of Tiger*, Elizabeth Marshall Thomas provides an explanation for the relative lack of evolutionary change in the design of cats since they first appeared in prehistory:

> In short, cats resemble each other because, so far, they have had no reason to change. Good hunters since the lynxlike Urcat of the Miocene from whom modern cats descend, the cats have had no need to adjust their bodies or their diets in response to major changes in the world's climate. Why not? Because unlike the diets of other animals, the diet of cats didn't change. The vegetarian menu listed everything from bananas to pecans, from seaweed to eucalyptus leaves, items so different from one another that completely different organisms were required to find, chew, and digest them, but the cat menu listed only one item: meat. From a cat's point of view, the difference between a bird who eats cherries, a fish who eats algae, and a giraffe who eats acacia thorns is mainly one of quantity. All three are meat, and a cat can benefit from any one of them if he can catch it. So while the glaciers came and went, while the vegetarians struggled against all odds trying to digest new plants and adapt themselves to overwhelming global changes, the cats simply kept on hunting, waiting to pounce on whoever managed to survive into the next epoch. The limber cat body that hunted successfully in the Pliocene hunts just as successfully today.

Scientific names are the only reliable indicator of the relationships between organisms. Common names can be extremely misleading in this regard. For example, there are three different species of big cat that have the word leopard as part of their common name: leopards, clouded leopards, and snow leopards. Despite similarities in appearance and behavior, individuals from one species cannot mate with other species and produce fertile offspring—the generally accepted standard by which all organisms are considered to be members of a species. Beyond being members of the subfamily Pantherinae, the three "leopard" species have little or no relationship to one another. The cat commonly called a leopard, *Panthera pardus*, is thought to be most closely related to the other large cats with which it shares its genus—the lion (*Panthera leo*), tiger (*Panthera tigris*), and jaguar (*Panthera onca*). The snow leopard, *Uncia uncia*, is different enough to occupy a genus all its own. Similarly, the clouded leopard, *Neofelis nebulosa*, is alone in its genus.

Leopards: Hunting specialists

No matter how they differ, leopards have a great deal in common. Under the skin, leopards are pretty much the same. Like every cat, nearly every part of a leopard's form is a reflection of its evolution as an animal that hunts and kills other animals for food.

Some of the most dramatic of these adaptations can be seen on the head of a leopard—or any other cat. For example, leopards have large, forward-facing eyes that serve as their primary tool for locating prey. Leopards' eyes are very sensitive to movement, allowing them to sense even a faint movement of grass or leaves as an animal passes by. The placement of the eyes on the front of the skull provides leopards with binocular vision, an indispensable tool for accurately judging distances when chasing and pouncing on prey.

In addition to their acute eyesight, leopards and other cats possess extremely sensitive hearing. Leopards can hear sounds of high frequency, an ability that serves them well for detecting the sounds of potential prey, whether it is moving through leaves or across the face of a rocky cliff.

The leopard uses its large, highly alert eyes to locate prey.

Like all cats, leopards can swivel their ears, allowing them to perceive sounds coming from any direction without moving their heads and potentially alerting their prey.

The face of a leopard and its cat kin is also remarkable for being much shorter than the faces of other carnivores. The shortened jaw allows leopards to deliver a very powerful bite. In addition, long, sharp canine teeth (or fangs) make it possible not only to grab and hold prey but also to kill prey outright by puncturing a major artery, the windpipe, or the brain. Leopards and other cats have fewer teeth than other carnivores do, but those teeth are particularly well suited to their job. Once its prey is dead, the leopard uses specialized molars to bite off pieces of meat. These teeth, called carnassials, have extremely sharp edges and function like the blades of scissors to cut through meat as the animal bites down. Cats, including leopards, do not chew their food; instead, pieces are bitten off and swallowed whole.

Leopards' bodies are designed for flexibility and speed, features that are important when chasing and attacking prey.

In addition to the adaptations found on a leopard's head and skull, there are many features of its body that are important for chasing and catching prey. Every cat's body is designed for flexibility; an extraordinarily flexible spine and freely moving shoulder blades allow leopards and other cats to stretch out their legs while running, adding speed as they attack. The posture of a leopard also enhances its speed and agility. Typical of cats (and many other animals that must chase their prey), leopards walk on their toes. This digitigrade posture serves to lengthen their legs, providing more running speed. The leopard's foot is also notable for housing sharp claws that can be pulled back, or retracted, into protective sheaths when not in use. Having retractable claws provides two main advantages. First, since they are not worn down by walking, the claws remain sharp for use in capturing prey. A leopard uses its sharp claws to grasp and steady its prey while delivering the fatal bite. Second, being able to retract its claws allows a leopard to move silently when stalking its prey, without betraying its presence by the sound of the claws contacting the ground.

The social life of leopards

Hunting, like most leopard behavior, is undertaken alone. Leopards are solitary creatures; unless they are a pair courting and breeding or females raising cubs, leopards spend most of their lives by themselves. Although they seldom meet face to face, leopards have several ways of communicating with one another, primarily through the use of scent. Leopards use urine, feces, and secretions from scent glands to convey a variety of information. One of the most important uses of scent marking is for proclaiming an individual leopard's territory. Typically, a male leopard will maintain a territory that encompasses that of one or more females and will mark his boundaries by spraying urine and raking his claws on trees. By defending this area from other males, the leopard will ensure that he has breeding opportunities with the females. A female leopard's scent marks allow the male to determine whether she is receptive to mating.

Although the breeding habits of the three leopard species are still largely unknown, scientists believe that their behavior is similar to that of other large cats, with the male and female leopards remaining together and mating repeatedly throughout the female's period of estrus, usually 7 to 10 days. After breeding, the pair likely separates to resume their solitary lives. After a gestation period of 90 to 105 days, the female produces a litter of two to four cubs. Although the cubs are small and helpless at birth, they grow rapidly and gain independence—in the case of the leopard and snow leopard, by the time they are a year and a half old. Clouded leopard cubs mature even more quickly and probably leave their mothers before their first birthday.

Specialized behavior

Although the biology of all wild cats is basically the same, the group is diverse in terms of the specialized adaptations and behavior each species possesses. Generally, cats are highly specialized for a particular habitat and lifestyle. The leopard, however, is unusual in its ability to thrive in a variety of habitat types. In fact, the leopard can be found throughout a large portion of the continents of both Africa and Asia. The leopard is considered to have the

Rearing Young

While studying leopards, biologist John Seidensticker had the opportunity to observe a female leopard that had just given birth to cubs. In the book *Great Cats* he describes the female's pattern of behavior during the cubs' first weeks.

My colleagues and I were able to follow the movements of a female leopard during the first six weeks after she gave birth. She moved her two cubs three times within a 25 hectare (62 acre) area of tall grass during this period. During the third week, the female stayed with the cubs for 33 hours, was gone for 36 hours, then returned and stayed for 29 hours. This pattern was repeated at six weeks of age. All told during these early weeks, she spent about half her time with or in the close vicinity of her young, and when she departed it was usually for more than 24 hours. . . . During this six-week period she used a home range of about 8 square kilometers (just over 3 square miles). She could cross it easily in two hours or less. Spending such long periods away from her young was evidently dictated not only by the time needed to hunt and kill her prey, but by the fact that once she made a kill she had to stay with the dead animal to protect it from scavengers and consume it before it decomposed (a quick process in hot, humid climates).

During the early weeks following birth, a female leopard often leaves her cubs to hunt for food.

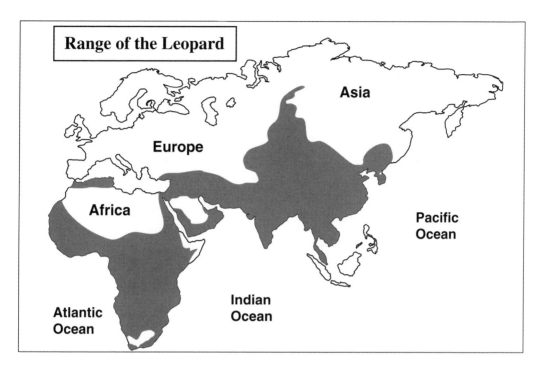

Range of the Leopard

Asia

Europe

Africa

Pacific
Ocean

Indian
Ocean

Atlantic
Ocean

widest distribution of any type of wild cat. The leopard's range extends across almost all of Africa south of the Sahara Desert, throughout India, parts of the Middle East, in most parts of Southeast Asia, and in the Russian Far East. In this enormous range, leopards can be found in a variety of habitats, including forests, grasslands, semideserts, and mountains. Leopards can survive in drastically different climates such as the hot, humid tropics found at the equator and the freezing, snowy forests of Siberia.

Because leopards have adapted to life in so many different places, scientists have recognized that leopards found in some regions are different enough from leopards in other regions to be classified in separate groups called subspecies. The designation of a subspecies may be based on the physical features of the cat, such as coat length and color; its geographic location; and genetic similarities determined by DNA analysis. This is an imprecise science, and the number of subspecies of leopards is currently in question. Once, scientists thought there might be as many as thirty leopard subspecies. Today, however, research

Black-coated leopards, generally known as panthers, are found mostly in forested areas.

indicates that many of these subspecies classifications are not justified and that there may be as few as eight subspecies. Some subspecies, though, are clearly recognized as being distinct, including the Amur leopard of Russia (*Panthera pardus orientalis*), the Sri Lankan leopard (*P. p. kotiya*), the Persian leopard (*P. p. saxicolor*) of Iran and Afghanistan, and the Arabian leopard (*P. p. nimr*).

No matter what subspecies they are, leopards vary widely in color, generally ranging from pale yellow to dark gold. The leopard's coat color is largely an adaptation to the specific terrain where it hunts. Leopards living in dry, semidesert areas, for example, tend to have almost cream-colored coats. Leopards living in the rain forest have coats of a deep gold that blends nicely with the patches of sunlight that find their way to the forest floor. Leopards can also have black coats. These leopards, generally known as panthers, but more correctly called melanistic, can be found wherever leopards range but are most common in forested areas. The background color on all leopards is covered by rings of spots called rosettes. Melanistic leopards also have rosettes, but they are faint and difficult to see.

Just as their coloration varies so, too, does the size of leopards. Wild leopards have been documented weighing from 70 to 200 pounds for males and 55 to 100 pounds for females. From the tip of its nose to the tip of its tail, a leopard measures 6 to 6.5 feet. The body size of the leopard is an important factor in this cat's adaptability. A leopard is small enough to sustain itself by capturing and consuming small prey, but it also has the size and strength necessary to capture large animals when they are available. For this reason, leopards are considered to be generalists—animals that can thrive in many environments by consuming many different types and sizes of prey. The leopard's menu consists of almost every sort of animal imaginable; more than ninety-two different types of prey have been recorded in Africa alone. They have been known to prey on animals as small as dung beetles or as large as a 1,900-pound hoofed animal called an eland. Other prey may include rodents, rabbits, monkeys, antelope, deer, giraffe calves, wild pigs, and foxes.

Often, after making a kill, a leopard will cache, or store, its food in the branches of a tree to avoid competition from other meat-eating animals intent on helping themselves to an easy meal. Storing a kill this way requires tremendous strength; a leopard can lug a carcass into a tree that is two to three times the cat's own weight. Feats of strength such as this have led to the leopard's reputation as being, pound for pound, the world's most powerful cat.

The snow leopard

While leopards are well adapted to life in equatorial forests and plains, snow leopards are ideally suited to life in the mountains. Snow leopards, in fact, are perfectly adapted to inhabit one of the harshest and most remote places on earth. They live in the high mountains and desert plateaus of twelve countries in Central Asia, including Nepal, Mongolia, China, Pakistan, India, and Russia. Snow leopards are usually found at elevations from 9,800 feet to as high as 18,000 feet, where they must contend with the challenges of surviving extremely cold temperatures.

The snow leopard has several specialized adaptations to cope with life in such a frigid environment. Its thick, soft, grayish-white coat keeps it warm even in freezing temperatures. Additional warmth is provided by the cat's long, furry tail that it wraps over its face while resting. The snow leopard's large paws serve as snowshoes, keeping it from sinking into deep snow as it travels along the mountain ridges.

In addition to its adaptations for surviving in a cold climate, the snow leopard is perfectly built for negotiating the steep, rugged cliffs that make up its mountain terrain. The snow leopard's tail, measuring nearly 3 feet long (almost half its body length), serves as a balancing tool as it roams narrow rock ledges and descends steep cliffs. It is also aided in rock climbing by relatively short front legs that give it stability and strength. Its hind legs are longer, providing spring-like power for leaping. In fact, the snow leopard is a record-holding athlete; it can leap 30 feet horizontally in one bound, farther than any other cat. The snow leopard's large paws spread out to help it gain better footholds while walking on the loose rocks and soil commonly found on the cliff faces.

Snow leopards' tendency to utilize rocky areas more frequently than areas of deep snow compelled snow leopard

researcher Rodney Jackson to comment on this species' misleading name: "Were it not for the beautiful and evocative sound of the words 'snow leopard,' I would be tempted to consider 'crag leopard' a more apt description. For one thing, leopard prey is usually found below the permanent snow line. But snow leopards have been known to cross 18,000 foot passes on occasion or meander across high glaciers as they move between major valleys."[1]

To survive in this harsh, barren land, snow leopards must be willing to eat virtually any kind of prey available, including yaks, pheasants, hares, and marmots. However, the snow leopard depends most heavily on hoofed animals for the bulk of its diet. A snow leopard is capable of killing an animal up to three times its own weight of 75 to 90 pounds (females) or 100 to 125 pounds (males). In most areas, the cat's primary prey is the bharal, or blue sheep. In addition, snow leopards will also hunt wild goats called ibex and markhor, a species of wild sheep called argali, and another hoofed animal called the Himalayan tahr. These animals are extremely alert, quick, and sure-footed, making the snow leopard's task of capturing one difficult.

Very few people have witnessed a wild snow leopard in pursuit of its prey. Snow leopard researcher Gary Ahlborn, however, had the extreme good fortune of being in the right place at the right time to make just such an observation. While gathering firewood for his expedition's camp in northwestern Nepal, Ahlborn spotted a herd of eleven bharal feeding. After watching them for twenty-five minutes, the action began. He recorded the event in his field notebook:

3:27 P.M.: Three rapid sets of warning chirps and I see a female [bharal] and lamb dart out from behind the knoll. Less than a second later one of the big males came plunging over the right side of the knoll, down the steep slope and directly toward me. Right behind him was a snow leopard. Both were traveling at top speed, taking huge strides. After a chase of about a hundred yards, the leopard made a quick lunge forward, catching the male on the left side of its rump with its left forepaw and jaw. This sent a cloud of pelage [hair] into the air. The bharal's rear dropped nearly to the ground and its knees buckled as it turned into the slope and absorbed the leopard's blow. The leopard's momentum forced it straight downslope, all its limbs off the ground and outstretched. Its long tail flung into the air and around to its left side, causing it to twist sidewinder-fashion in the direction of the bharal and regain its control. The bharal made several more direction changes, then just above a large boulder it again turned sharply into the slope. The leopard, not able to turn quickly enough, went over the top of the boulder, spun halfway around, and landed in a spray of fine soil several yards beyond. After it regained its footing it walked in the direction of the fleeing bharal, sat down, and licked its forepaws and the air in front of its nose.[2]

Although many hunting attempts may end with the escape of the intended victim, like the one observed by Ahlborn, evidence from snow leopard kills and researchers' calculations of snow leopard energy requirements indicate that snow leopards successfully capture a large prey animal every ten to fifteen days. This figure translates to a cat killing twenty to thirty adult bharal every year, a dramatic testament to the snow leopard's hunting expertise.

 ## First Glimpse of the Snow Leopard

In 1971, *National Geographic* published the first photographs ever taken of a snow leopard in the wild. Accompanying the photos was biologist George Schaller's recollection of the moment he first saw a snow leopard:

Suddenly I saw the snow leopard. Wisps of cloud moved between us, and she became a ghost creature, appearing and disappearing as if in a dream. We were 120 feet apart on a rugged Pakistani cliff, neither of us moving—two being bound to each other in a world of swirling snow. Thus, last December, I glimpsed one of the rarest and least known of the world's great cats. . . .

The fluffy tail of this female, almost the length of her yard-long body, seemed to assume a life of its own when she moved. But her eyes were her most extraordinary feature. Pale, with a frosty glitter softened only by a tinge of amber, they were the eyes of a creature used to immense solitudes and snowy wastes.

The clouded leopard

Until recently, details like those about the habits of the snow leopard in the wild were unavailable. Although a great deal still remains to be discovered, scientific studies conducted since the early 1980s have revealed much about the lives of these cats. In contrast, scientists are struggling to gain even the most basic knowledge about wild clouded leopards. Virtually nothing is known about their biology and behavior in their natural habitat. Most of what scientists do know about clouded leopards is a result of research carried out with animals living in captivity. Studying clouded leopards in their native environment is extremely difficult for many reasons. The heat, humidity, and discomfort of conducting studies in the tropical forest are challenges that many researchers are not willing to endure. In addition, the vegetation in the forest makes it difficult to track or spot cats. Even if spotting a clouded leopard were easier, the shy, secretive nature of this cat would likely cause it to quickly flee, making close observation impossible. Finally, clouded leopards are thought to spend a great deal of time in the trees, further reducing any chances of sighting one.

Named for the cloudlike oblong markings on its brownish-gray coat, the clouded leopard is known for its highly arboreal, or tree-climbing, lifestyle. The clouded leopard is a feline acrobat; it is capable of climbing headfirst down a tree, traveling along horizontal branches by clinging to them upside down, and even dangling from branches by only its hind feet. The clouded leopard has a number of adaptations that contribute to its remarkable skill as a climber. It has a long, thickly furred tail that serves as a counterbalance while moving through the trees. This tail is nearly 3 feet long and makes up half the total length of the adult cat. Clouded leopards also have very short legs, giving them a rather squat appearance. These shortened limbs provide the animal with the leverage and power necessary to easily pull themselves up through the branches.

Adult clouded leopards range in weight from 35 to 45 pounds for males and from 25 to 35 pounds for females.

A clouded leopard has remarkable climbing abilities due to its long tail and short legs.

Although clouded leopards are not as large as leopards, snow leopards, or other big cats, they do share some common characteristics with them. In particular, they have large skulls containing very large teeth. The clouded leopard has the largest canine teeth in proportion to body size of any species of cat. These canines can be as long as 1.75 inches and have a very sharp back edge. The great length of the clouded leopard's canines has led to its being compared with the now-extinct saber-toothed cat. The reason for these extra-long teeth is unknown; however, biologists speculate that they may be an adaptation for either killing large-hoofed prey, such as deer and wild pigs, or piercing the skulls of monkeys, the favored prey for these cats.

Clouded leopards can be found in the tropical forests, mangrove swamps, and scrub areas throughout most of Southeast Asia, including Sumatra, Borneo, Malaysia, Thailand, and Myanmar (Burma), as well as southern China,

Nepal, and eastern India. Clouded leopards used to inhabit the island of Taiwan, but a confirmed sighting has not occurred since the 1960s, so they are generally believed to be extinct in that location.

Disappearing leopards

Even though little is known about clouded leopards in the wild, one thing is clear: Their numbers, along with those of leopards and snow leopards, are declining. Because of the cat's reclusive habits, estimates for clouded leopard population numbers do not exist, but evidence indicates that some areas that once supported clouded leopards are no longer inhabited by these cats. Snow leopard numbers are also difficult to estimate with accuracy, but studies completed so far indicate that thirty-five hundred to seven thousand individuals remain.

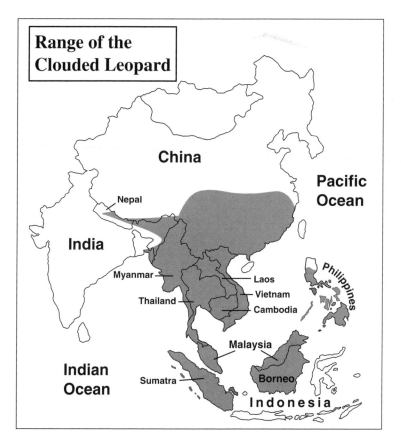

Leopards range over such an extended area that generalizations about their populations are impossible. It is thought that leopard populations in sub-Saharan Africa are currently fairly stable, and these cats are generally not considered endangered, with populations perhaps numbering 500,000. In Asia, some leopard populations have increased while others have decreased; some are nearly extinct. For example, the Amur leopard is one of the world's rarest cats, with approximately forty individuals remaining in Russia. The Arabian leopard has also suffered a severe population decline and now numbers only one hundred.

Whatever their current status, all three species of leopards are exceedingly vulnerable to human pressures, which are responsible for their declining numbers. As human populations expand further and the leopards' natural ranges shrink, leopards must either adapt to living close to people or disappear.

2

Habitat Loss

THE WORLD'S POPULATION today is more than 6 billion, and estimates by the United Nations indicate this figure will reach 7.9 to 10.9 billion by the year 2025. This rapid growth in human numbers is increasingly taking its toll on the earth's wilderness areas. Today, few places remain truly wild. Almost all animal habitats have experienced varying degrees of human encroachment (the moving in of people and their associated activities). One of the most dramatic results of such encroachment is the accelerating rate of deforestation as more and more people cut down forests to obtain building materials, create farmland, and obtain fuel for cooking and heating.

At greatest risk from this conversion of wilderness to human settlement are tropical forests, which are home to many of the world's wild leopards. Southeast Asia, in particular, is undergoing some of the highest rates of deforestation in the world. In just a single decade, between 1981 and 1990, Southeast Asia lost nearly 15 percent of its forests, the greatest loss of any region on earth.

Much of this deforestation is the result of people working to provide basic necessities for their families and communities. People cut down trees to use as firewood, they clear forests to create farmland, and they cut trees to earn relatively modest incomes. In addition to human subsistence activities, commercial ventures such as logging and the creation of palm oil and rubber plantations also contribute greatly to tropical deforestation. For example, since the 1960s, Asia has led the world in tropical timber harvest.

In Malaysia alone, more than eighteen thousand square miles of forest, one-quarter of that country's original forested area, has been converted to plantations.

Not only is the total forest area being dramatically reduced, but around the world forest areas have become very fragmented. In other words, instead of existing in large, unbroken tracts, the forests are small and separated from one another. Tropical Asia suffers from forest fragmentation to a greater extent than any other region. Only 3 percent of its forested land still remains in undeveloped blocks of significant size.

Deforestation in countries such as Malaysia has caused great habitat loss for leopard populations.

How deforestation affects the three leopard species is a matter of debate among experts. In their book *Wild Cats*, Kristin Nowell and Peter Jackson provide an overview of the limited studies that have taken place on wild cats' response to habitat loss. They suggest that the overall effects are perhaps less serious than was previously thought: "Although habitat loss is often described as the primary threat to cat populations, there are several indications that cats adjust relatively well to many forms of habitat loss and fragmentation, including deforestation, with only extremes such as urban settlement being generally devoid of cats. Most cats make use of a variety of habitats, and this not only buffers them against the loss of a preferred habitat type, but also suggests substantial flexibility in habitat selection and use."[3] Simply put, cats in general have proven adaptable.

Adapting to change

As evidence for cats' ability to use altered habitat, Nowell and Jackson cite a study in which a researcher recorded the presence of clouded leopards and several species of small wild cats in Asian forests where logging had occurred as little as one year previously. They suggest that it can be stated that "the only type of habitats not suitable for cats are those which have inadequate or unsuitable cover and prey (and water)."[4]

As Nowell and Jackson claim, a cat's ability to be able to hunt its natural prey is key to its survival, no matter what the state of its habitat. If a cat's prey is able to flourish in a habitat, even a degraded one, then it is likely the cat will flourish as well. However, if the habitat is so badly damaged that prey cannot survive, cats will disappear or be forced into conflicts with people. For this reason, it is vital that some habitat areas are protected. Further research will allow scientists to gain a better understanding of ways this can be accomplished.

Nowell and Jackson summarize the situation:

> "Cats are wide-ranging and thinly distributed, and for most it will be impossible to protect all but a small proportion of their historic ranges. It is encouraging that cats are among the more

Threatened Leopards

According to the 2000 IUCN Red List of Threatened Species, the following species and subspecies are considered at risk in the wild.

Common Name	Scientific Name	Status
Amur Leopard	*Panthera pardus orientalis*	Critically Endangered
Anatolian Leopard	*Panthera pardus tulliana*	Critically Endangered
Clouded Leopard	*Neofelis nebulosa*	Vulnerable
Javan Leopard	*Panthera pardus melas*	Endangered
North African Leopard	*Panthera pardus panthera*	Critically Endangered
North Chinese Leopard	*Panthera pardus japonensis*	Endangered
North Persian Leopard	*Panthera pardus saxicolor*	Endangered
Snow Leopard	*Uncia uncia*	Endangered
South Arabian Leopard	*Panthera pardus nimr*	Critically Endangered
Sri Lankan Leopard	*Panthera pardus kotiya*	Endangered

adaptable species which are capable of coping rather well with the changes that the growing human population is making to the world environment. Human settlement, activity, and development are not necessarily inimical [hostile] to cats. Future efforts need to be directed towards understanding to what degree cat species tolerate habitat loss, fragmentation, and modification; developing guidelines as to how land use can be modified to allow cats to persist; and finding ways to reduce persecution of cats (especially the big cats) in habitat used by humans."[5]

Habitat loss and the Amur leopard

Although scientists disagree about how habitat loss and alteration affect leopards living in some parts of the world, researchers believe that the degraded habitats' effects on the Amur leopard are much more clear. Also known as the Far Eastern leopard, the Amur leopard is the most endangered subspecies of leopard and is quite possibly the rarest of all the world's wild cats. Although Amur leopards once roamed throughout northeastern China, the Korean peninsula, and the Russian Far East, now only a few of the animals remain. Between forty and forty-four individuals are confined to a small area of Russia between the city of Vladivostok and the Chinese border. An unknown number of Amur leopards also remain in North Korea, but this population may amount to just a handful of individuals. A recent survey in the northern Chinese province of Jilin indicated that four to seven cats live there—a decline from forty-five cats in 1976. In the northern part of China's Heilongjiang province along the Amur River, for which the cat is named, there have been no reports of Amur leopards for seventy to eighty years.

The Amur leopard suffered declining populations from habitat loss as human encroachment took place throughout the last century. People were attracted to the region for its rich natural resources, such as timber, minerals, wild game, and fur-bearing animals. Clear-cutting eliminated huge tracts of forest where Amur leopards once ranged, and overhunting of deer and wild boar reduced their available prey. These problems remain today, especially as a result of the declining

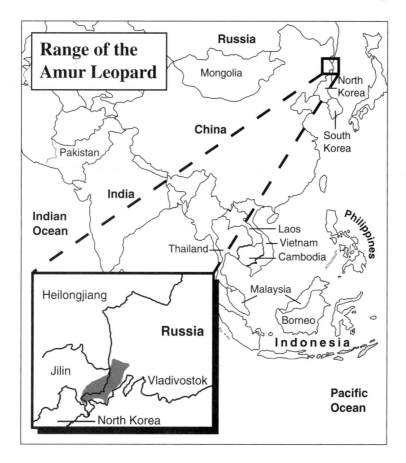

Russian economy. To generate much-needed income, Russia has sold logging and mining rights in this region, which will result in even more habitat loss for the Amur leopard.

The most dramatic example of how habitat disruption has adversely affected Amur leopards occurred within the last twenty-five years. Development in an area north of Vladivostok split what had once been a single population of Amur leopards into three parts. Since that split, two of the populations have become extinct as further development destroyed their habitat. The population that remains, along the Chinese border, likely only survived because territorial disputes between China and Russia limited development. As relations between China and Russia improve, scientists are concerned that development in this region might soon expand, resulting in the extinction of the remaining Amur leopards in the area.

Even without more development, these cats are feeling the effects of human encroachment. Today, the forests where the Amur leopards live are almost totally surrounded by farms and villages. On the Chinese side of the border, most of the suitable leopard habitat has been converted to fields where rice or soybeans are grown. On the Russian side, farmers use fire extensively to manage their croplands. By burning their fields in the fall and winter, they hope to increase the soil's fertility. These fires, however, often spread into the adjacent forests and cause such severe damage that there is no food available for deer and other herbivores. As these animals disappear, the Amur leopards are left with no prey. In some areas, this repeated cycle of burning and forest destruction has resulted in the transformation of what was once suitable forest habitat for leopards into grasslands where the cats cannot survive.

The snow leopard's fragmented habitat

Just as the Amur leopard has experienced dramatic population declines as a result of human settlement so, too, has the snow leopard. The snow leopard's range stretches widely over the high mountains and desert plateaus of Central Asia. Until relatively recently, very few people oc-

cupied this region. Today, however, the human population is expanding here, and people are moving into areas where the snow leopard once lived undisturbed. Although the snow leopard's range is still vast, it has become fragmented into much smaller, isolated pieces.

As is true for the Amur leopard, one challenge for the snow leopard is the dramatic loss of its natural prey near where villages have been established. In some cases, this is from the overgrazing of the mountain grasslands by domestic sheep and goats kept by villagers. When the hillsides are overgrazed, the wild goats and sheep that the snow leopard relies on for food drop in numbers. Furthermore, these wild goats and sheep are a source of meat for villagers, and overhunting of the prey populations places additional pressure on snow leopards. In one study undertaken in China, for example, a researcher counted only

A herd of sheep in Central Asia. Overgrazing by domestic sheep and goats has resulted in a scarcity of prey for the leopard.

eleven ibex in a ninety-five-square-mile area that was previously known for supporting a large ibex population. When their prey disappears, snow leopards will disappear as well. Because so many areas throughout Central Asia no longer provide suitable habitat for snow leopards, the cats that remain are becoming increasingly isolated from one another in smaller and smaller populations.

Dangers of small population size

The shrinking size of these snow leopard and Amur leopard populations places them at increasing risk of the threats faced by any species under similar conditions. Disease is a serious concern to any animal group with low numbers; a single epidemic can kill so many individuals that the population might never recover. Likewise, a natural disaster could also inflict serious damage to the group. Of most concern to scientists, however, is a much more subtle danger—decreasing genetic diversity.

When a group of animals becomes isolated, for any reason, individuals are no longer able to leave or enter the population as they could under normal circumstances. Without this genetic migration, as this coming and going of breeding animals is known, over time all the individuals in the group share the same pool of genes, essentially becoming more closely related to one another. When these closely related individuals breed, known as inbreeding, birth defects that jeopardize the health of their offspring show up in greater numbers. If these defects are serious and occur often enough, the health of the entire population declines.

The most common results of inbreeding are decreased fertility and a reduced survival rate for the young. One study of the effects of inbreeding on captive mammals demonstrated that offspring survival declined by almost one-third when a brother and sister bred. Such declines in the survival rate of offspring of isolated groups of wild leopards could put the entire population at risk of extinction. Although researchers have not yet observed problems caused by inbreeding in wild leopard populations, many worry that inbreeding could eventually become a serious concern as populations decrease in size.

Scientists who are concerned about inbreeding in wild animal populations must determine the minimum breeding population size necessary to maintain a species' genetic health. The number of breeding animals needed to maintain an appropriate level of genetic diversity for a certain period of time, usually at least one hundred years, is called a minimum viable population (MVP). Because not all animals in a population are breeding animals, the actual number of animals needed to achieve the MVP is substantially higher. For example, scientists estimate that for wild cats to have an MVP of several hundred breeding animals, the actual population needs to be almost one thousand individuals.

Protecting leopard habitat

The large population necessary to ensure the long-term survival of leopard species highlights a major challenge of wild cat conservation. Maintaining habitat for this many individuals requires setting aside huge areas of suitable land, which is unlikely to happen in regions of high human population and heavy development. Fortunately, however, the amount of land set aside as national parks and reserves in countries where leopards live is on the rise. The leaders of countries all around the world are taking a more active role in preserving their nations' natural heritage by giving legal protection to areas important for conserving plants and animals. As of 1992, more than 6 percent of Asia's tropical rain forest was receiving legal protection in the form of 865 nature reserves.

One of the newest nature reserves in Asia was designed to protect the northeastern forest home of Amur leopards and another endangered big cat, the Amur (Siberian) tiger. Established in December 2001, the Chinese Huichun Natural Reserve covers thirty-six thousand acres along the Chinese-Russian border. The creation of this reserve played a vital role in expanding the available habitat for the leopards in this region. Also important was the recognition by the governments of both China and Russia that the area along their shared border is one of critical conservation importance. Liu Yongfan of China's State Forestry Administration says, "China's newly released master plan for wildlife and protected areas has listed transboundary protected areas in Jilin and Heilongjiang as top conservation priorities."[6] A Chinese conservationist, Endi Zhang, goes on to note that by providing protection for wild cats and their prey, "We have a great opportunity to demonstrate how recovery of endangered species can be done in China."[7]

 ## National Parks in Africa

In their book *The Myth of Wild Africa*, Jonathan Adams and Thomas McShane discuss the problems associated with the establishment of traditional parks and reserves in Africa.

Despite the accomplishments and the goodwill, as long as conservation operates on the notion that saving wild animals means keeping them as far away as possible from human beings, it will become less and less relevant to modern Africans. Parks and other protected areas will eventually be overrun by people's need for land unless the parks serve, or are at least not completely inimical [hostile] to, the needs of the local population.

The method for establishing parks has hardly changed in over a century. The process has always involved the expensive operation of removing those people living on the newly protected land. In almost all cases, the result is a park surrounded by people who were excluded from the planning of the area, do not understand its purpose, derive little or no benefit from the money poured into its creation, and hence do not support its existence. As a result, local communities develop a lasting distrust of park authorities, in part because of the glaring lack of attention those authorities, supported by conservationists, have traditionally paid to the link between park ecology, the survival of wildlife, and the livelihood of the displaced people.

Turning interest into action, however, is often difficult. Although many countries have expressed a desire to establish reserves, they are often limited by a lack of money or experience to develop them properly. Priscilla Allen of the International Snow Leopard Trust, a conservation group working to safeguard wild snow leopards, describes the situation in Mongolia: "The Mongolian government has a very good commitment to conservation. They have committed to put 30 percent of Mongolia's entire land under a protected basis, which is very ambitious. They already have about 10 percent."[8] Even though Mongolia has made the commitment to protecting its wildlife, the trust's conservation director, Tom McCarthy, admits that challenges exist: "You can identify all the protected areas you want but the fact is, Mongolia doesn't have the financial ability or expertise or the capacity to manage those reserves in any reasonable fashion right now."[9]

To protect the Amur leopard population, new reserves have been set up in the forests along the Chinese-Russian border.

Development and Conservation

Can human activities and conservation ever be compatible? In their book *The Myth of Wild Africa*, Jonathan Adams and Thomas McShane argue that they must if conservation is to be successful.

The most tenacious of all the old-fashioned ideas among conservationists holds that development is the enemy because of the technology it produces—roads, dams, irrigated farms, and the like. The unspoken message is that for conservation to succeed, it has to hold back the clock. That approach had some success before human population growth and human needs began to press in on even the remotest areas. To their credit, many conservationists now realize that erecting barricades from which to make a last desperate stand against development will fail. Success lies instead in understanding that conservation and development, long at loggerheads, are two parts of a single process. Conservation cannot ignore the needs of human beings, while development that runs roughshod over the environment is doomed. . . . Conservation will either contribute to solving the problems of the rural poor who live day to day with wild animals, or those animals will disappear.

The management of reserves is an important issue, for simply designating a piece of land as a protected area will do nothing to actually safeguard the plants and animals living there. People living on the edges of reserves commonly enter to collect firewood, harvest timber, graze cattle, or hunt. In some cases, the boundaries of parks are ignored completely as squatters move in and settle on the land. For example, the Sanjay Gandhi National Park in India has experienced a loss of more than three hundred acres of its land to squatters. Those who settle such land illegally often have no other option. The high land prices in the area have forced the growing number of people to make new settlements within the park's boundaries. This type of land use in protected areas will continue unless governments are able to adequately fund enforcement efforts and help provide better housing opportunities for their people.

In some cases, reserves are of limited effectiveness, no matter how well managed they might be. Although the establishment of parks and reserves is an important step, most of the reserves that have been created are too small to protect entire leopard populations. For example, there are no protected areas large enough to wholly contain breeding populations of snow leopards. As a result, only 35 percent of these cats are believed to live in areas where the habitat is considered protected. Likewise, the vast majority of leopards and clouded leopards live outside of protected areas.

One way to improve the effectiveness of land conservation in maintaining leopard populations over long periods of time is to make use of wildlife corridors. Wildlife corridors are strips of natural habitat that form connections

A snow leopard on a reserve. Only 35 percent of the snow leopard population live in protected areas.

The Value of Wildlife Corridors

Kristin Nowell and Peter Jackson explore the idea of wildlife corridors in their book *Wild Cats: Status Survey and Conservation Action Plan.*

Corridors have attracted much attention in the wake of growing awareness of the vulnerability of small isolated populations, and because the concept of linkages between larger blocks of habitat makes sense intuitively. A corridor strategy, according to one of its chief proponents, consists of maintaining or restoring natural landscape connectivity, not building connections between naturally isolated habitats. Because of their range requirements, large carnivores, particularly cats, are often used as examples of species which would benefit from corridors. . . . However, corridor strategies have been criticized because of the potential expense of purchasing narrow pieces of land in the vicinity of settlement or development (the same amount of money could buy more land in more remote areas). Critics further point to a lack of species-specific research documenting use vs. non-use of habitat corridors.

between reserves. Such corridors allow animals to move between protected areas and still remain in suitable habitat, instead of being exposed to more developed areas where they would be likely to have conflicts with people. The fact that a cat can enter or leave a previously isolated piece of habitat greatly increases the opportunity for genetic migration to occur, thereby keeping the genetic diversity of the population at a healthy level.

Regardless of the protection leopards receive through the establishment of specially designated reserves or by being recognized as endangered species, as the human population grows, these cats are coming into more frequent contact—and conflict—with people. When such conflict occurs, the ultimate loser is usually the leopard.

3

Conflicts Between Leopards and People

IT IS CLEAR that, in many cases, human encroachment has reduced the number of areas where leopards are able to live, but loss of habitat is not the only challenge facing these cats in their struggle for survival. In fact, it is the increasing contact with people brought about by encroachment that has now become the primary threat to leopards. Even when reserves are established, inevitably, some leopards leave the confines of protected areas, and when they do they often come into conflict with their human neighbors. Of course, leopards living outside of reserves must cope with these conflicts even more frequently. All too often, these clashes between people and leopards end tragically for both.

Leopard attacks on people

The most serious clashes occur when leopards attack people. Big cats occasionally kill and sometimes eat humans. The reasons an otherwise reclusive animal becomes a threat to humans vary. Sometimes a wild cat will attack people because it has been injured and is unable to hunt its natural prey. Other times, the reasons for attacks are not as clear. Biologists speculate that in some cases the cat was startled, mistook the human for another animal, or had no natural prey available.

Although lions and tigers are most notorious for attacking people, the leopard is also known for its occasional

Villagers in India display a man-eating leopard that was killed after it attacked at least six people.

aggression toward humans. In most places where leopards live, attacks on humans are rare, and more often the result of accidental encounters. However, there are many accounts from both Africa and Asia of deliberate attacks. A leopard that turns to killing people, commonly known as a man eater, is generally more feared than even the tiger because of its extreme boldness. Leopards are known for entering villages, going into houses, and even taking a victim from a room full of sleeping people without awakening others.

Records also suggest that when a leopard does begin attacking people, it continues to do so. One famous man-eating leopard in India killed 125 people from 1918 to 1926 before finally being shot. And in the region surrounding Sanjay Gandhi National Park, officials documented 14 deaths and 15 injuries as a result of leopard attacks from 1986 to 1996. Although this number of deaths in one region

 ## Man-Eating leopards

In the book *Great Cats: Majestic Creatures of the Wild* (edited by John Seidensticker and Susan Lumpkin), Charles McDougal describes the history of a man-eating leopard in India.

Perhaps the most notorious wild animal that ever lived was the man-eating leopard of Rudyaprayag. Between 1918 and 1926 it terrorized the route along which thousands of pilgrims annually ascended through the Garhwal Hills on their way to the Hindu shrines in the Himalayas, claiming 125 lives. This cat had the proverbial nine lives. Because its exploits were closely followed by the press, and questions even asked about it in the British House of Commons, no effort was spared to terminate its career, and a sizeable reward was placed on its head. Once it escaped when caught in a box trap, and again when sealed up in a cave—the entrance was opened by an incredulous local dignitary whereupon the leopard burst through the crowd of 500 people that had gathered outside. It survived various types of poison, trip-guns set over kills, and a fusillade of bullets fired by two British officers who ambushed it crossing a suspension bridge. Once the jaws of a powerful spring trap snapped shut on the leopard's foreleg but caught it at the very point where one of the trap's metal teeth had accidentally been broken off on the trip up; the cat was able to extricate itself before the hunters arrived. "The best hated and most feared animal in all India," the large, old male was finally shot by Jim Corbett after a hunt that lasted months. Sixteen years earlier Corbett had killed the Panar man-eater, a leopard that claimed 400 victims but received far less publicity.

is alarming, it pales in comparison to the conflicts between leopards and people to the north in the Himalayan foothills of Uttar Pradesh. Here, leopard attacks have long been common. For example, between 1988 and 2000, 141 people were killed. Both in Sanjay Gandhi National Park and in Uttar Pradesh, most of the victims were children under the age of fifteen. In addition, in Uttar Pradesh, 66 percent of the victims were women or girls. These statistics reflect the fact that women and their children do most of the work in the forests and fields and therefore are at greater risk of encountering a leopard.

Statistics also suggest that the problem of leopard attacks appears to be worsening. Indian researcher Dr. S.P. Goyal studied the human-leopard conflict in Uttar Pradesh and offers several possible explanations:

Because women and children do most of the forest work in Uttar Pradesh, they are at greater risk of leopard attacks than the men of the village.

 **The Leopard's Adaptability**

In the book *Great Cats*, biologist John Seidensticker relates a story that dramatically illustrates leopards' ability to adapt to the presence of people.

Just how adept leopards are at living in the forest-village interface became apparent in Nepal when scientists radio-tracked a leopard into a village one night. The leopard appeared to be trying to capture a goat from the herd kept in a village shed. Daylight came before the leopard could make a kill or retreat from the village. Caught away from any lane of escape, the cat spent the day in a woodpile amidst the hustle and bustle of daily village life. No one in the village—not even the dogs—knew it was there. The following night, it escaped. Leopards live in the suburbs of Nairobi and other African cities, much as coyotes live in the suburbs of Los Angeles, or foxes and raccoons live in the middle of Washington, D.C.

In the past, leopards rarely turned man-eater but now the situation is different as they are killing humans throughout the year. [The] increase in higher frequencies of leopard-human conflicts during [the] last decade may be due to accelerating trends in habitat fragmentation, decline in potential habitats, scarcity of wild prey base, predominantly feeding on domestic species [which] leads [leopards] to come more closely to humans and to some extent may be due to [the] increase of [the] local leopard population. . . . Local villagers opined that in the past, leopards were timid by nature but now they are frequently roaming in the area even in day time and often stray into villages and towns in the search of prey. A change in leopard behavior to become extremely bold has been noticed due to habitat disturbance and loss of prey species.[10]

Biologists Kristin Nowell and Peter Jackson note that attacks occur most frequently near reserves where leopards are protected and offer a theory as to why this is: "Big cat attacks are perhaps most likely to occur in settled areas bordering protected populations of cats. A healthy population will include a dispersing class of both sub-adult animals seeking to establish a territory, and older former residents which have lost theirs. Both of these types of cats are prime candidates for becoming problem animals: the sub-adults have immature hunting skills, and the hunting efficiency of older animals is declining."[11]

Not surprisingly, local residents react to a man-eating cat by trying to kill it. In Uttar Pradesh, where people have endured the killing of so many members of their communities, ninety-three leopards were killed in the past twelve years, many by poisoning. These were the official numbers; the actual unreported figure is likely much higher. Local wildlife authorities work to control problem animals by capturing them for placement in zoos or killing them if no captive placement is possible.

Although it is well known that leopards occasionally attack people, this is not the case with clouded leopards and snow leopards. The only documented case of a clouded leopard attacking a person occurred in Burma in 1927. This incident involved a clouded leopard that sprang at a boy while he was cutting wood. The boy was able to kill the cat with a knife blow to its head. For their part, snow leopards have never been known to attack a person. In fact, snow leopards are known for being fairly submissive when encountered by people. Villagers have been able to chase them off of kills and even to throw stones at cornered cats without the snow leopards' fighting back.

Leopard predation on livestock

Although snow leopards are not known to pose a direct danger to people, one source of conflict is the animals' reputation in certain areas for killing livestock. In fact, attacks on livestock are an increasing problem. Often, the domestic animals, which are vulnerable and easy to kill, are an irresistible temptation to predators seeking a meal. Moreover, in some cases, livestock is the only food source remaining for leopards whose wild prey have disappeared.

Worldwide, wild cat predation on livestock is actually very low, resulting in losses of less than 1 to 3 percent of animals each year. However, in certain areas losses can be significant. In one region of western Nepal, for example, snow leopards killed seventy-two animals in just one year. Although the value of animals lost was only about $38 per family, that figure amounted to almost a third of the average annual family income of $122.

Even more disturbing than incidences of snow leopards killing a single goat, sheep, or yak for food are occasions when snow leopards kill many animals at a time, a situation known as surplus killing. Herders pen their flocks together in corrals overnight, and snow leopards that enter can wreak havoc. In Tibet, a snow leopard once killed 107 sheep in a single night. In India, a snow leopard entered a night corral and killed 53 sheep and goats.

Scientists have no explanation for surplus killing, but they have direct knowledge of how such behavior can devastate a person who relies on his animals for his living. Madan Oli, a researcher studying snow leopards in western Nepal, observed firsthand the effects livestock predation had on one local herdsman:

> With tears in his eyes, Anfe explained how worried he had been when 11 of his goats failed to return. The sun had already disappeared behind the horizon and the herdsman knew it would be pitch-black in less than an hour. He did not have a flashlight, so he decided he would wait until morning to search. But he slept very little that night, for he could guess what had happened to his goats. At the first rays of daylight, Anfe ate a breakfast . . . and then proceeded toward the site where he had last seen his goats. It was not long before he discovered that all the goats were dead. From the wounds it was obvious they had been killed by snow leopards. It took him about an hour to recover the carcasses. One of the goats had been completely consumed, another partially eaten. Nothing, or only small portions, had been eaten from the others. He collected the carcasses and carried home as many as he could. Later, he sent two of his daughters to fetch the rest. The news worried Anfe's wife, who had been planning to pay off part of the family debt by selling some of the goats. And his youngest daughter started to cry when she realized her father could not afford to buy her the dress he had promised.[12]

Faced with the possibility of this sort of economic hardship, it is not surprising that local people often have very strong negative feelings about snow leopards. As part of his research, Oli surveyed villagers to determine their views:

> The snow leopard's endangered status means nothing to the people of Manang. To them, leopards are vermin. It was not surprising that 95 percent of the local people had strong negative attitudes, and the majority of them considered predation losses to have exceeded tolerable levels. Ninety-seven percent suggested eradication of snow leopards as a suitable way of reducing their losses, of which 52 percent believed that was the only feasible method. At least five snow leopards have been killed in retaliation during the past ten years. In fact, snow leopards are killed throughout their range by herdsman.[13]

Reducing livestock predation

Although laws generally prohibit the killing of leopards and snow leopards, when predation on livestock escalates in an area, laws are often overlooked. To protect their livelihood, people will kill livestock predators at every op-

A farmer in Nepal oversees her goat pen. Leopard attacks on livestock cause serious financial hardship to farmers.

portunity. This type of persecution may be the final downfall for leopards living outside of protected areas.

Recognizing that leopards will inevitably kill livestock on occasion, conservationists believe the key to leopards' survival lies in eliminating the necessity for killing a problem cat. In many cases, the first step in resolving a conflict with a livestock predator is to identify the specific cat responsible and remove it. Even if the problem animal must be killed, dealing promptly with the situation may save other leopards in the process. Sometimes, too, a livestock killer can be captured and relocated to a more remote area.

Removal of a livestock predator may be helpful in the short term, but a longer-term solution is to improve livestock management to minimize the risk the animals face from predators. Many conservationists are now working with people in regions where leopard predation losses are high to help them find ways to keep their livestock safer.

Conservationists have identified specific actions that have been found to be effective in reducing the incidence of livestock losses by discouraging attacks by cats. One action is to provide guards or guard dogs to watch over the herds as they graze. Another is to choose grazing areas that are out in the open, away from areas with cover, which are preferred by predators. One of the most important actions is to construct predator-proof enclosures to contain the livestock at night, when the risk of attack is highest.

Compensating livestock losses

Despite these efforts to improve livestock management, some animals will inevitably be killed by leopards. To encourage herders to tolerate these losses, many governments and conservation organizations have begun a practice of compensating them, or paying damages, for animals killed by cats. One place where a compensation plan has been established is in the Russian Far East. Here, predation on livestock by Amur leopards is a serious concern. The region is home to several thousand deer living on farms, where they are raised for their antlers, which are sold for use in traditional Asian medicines. Twenty-seven animals on two farms

A man holds the horns of a sheep killed by a leopard. Conservationists are working with farmers to ensure the safety of their livestock.

were killed between September 1999 and August 2001, by either Amur leopards or Amur tigers, which also live in the region. However, these losses were compensated by payments to the farmers by a Dutch conservation organization, the Tigris Foundation. In addition to compensation for their losses, the farmers here are also paid $80 per month for the very presence of each leopard living near their land. With this type of encouragement, it is likely that the local people will be more receptive to sharing their land with leopards.

India's compensation programs

Another place where a compensation program has been established is Hemis National Park in northwestern India. This park is considered excellent snow leopard habitat and supports thirty to fifty cats and an abundance of prey. However, nearly sixteen hundred people live either within the park or in nearby villages; they face serious losses of their livestock from predators. From January 1998 to February

1999, predators killed 492 animals in the area. More than half of these losses were attributable to snow leopards. The animals taken represent a loss of $23,500 to the people of the villages. The park's wildlife authorities have a program, established in 1994, to compensate for these losses, but so far the results have been mixed. Because losses have been so high, compensation has consumed as much as half of the wildlife department's budget each year, making it difficult for the department to fulfill other obligations. Furthermore, the payments made to villagers represent only a fraction of the animals' true market value, and villagers must walk long distances to make a claim. The result is a lack of enthusiasm for the compensation program and a temptation for the villagers to hunt down and kill the snow leopards rather than accept further losses.

Compensation programs managed by individual state governments have encountered similar problems elsewhere in India. To certify that a farmer's claim is authentic, a number of reporting guidelines must be followed, including an investigation of the incident by a wildlife official. Because of the amount of bureaucratic red tape involved, many farmers hesitate to file claims. One study of the effectiveness of livestock compensation reported by Nowell and Jackson in their book *Wild Cats* examined some of the challenges of these programs: "The problems they cited included low level of compensation in comparison to the purchase price of replacement animals; excessive travel to report losses; the likelihood that an official would not be available to register a report of livestock predation within the mandatory reporting period (24 hours); subjective assessments by officials of the worth of predated livestock; and difficulties associated with receiving payment for settlements."[14] For compensation programs to be truly effective in encouraging people to try to coexist with wild cats, these challenges will have to be overcome.

Commercial hunting of leopards

Although many people are motivated to kill leopards and other wild cats out of fear for their own safety or that of their livestock, others kill them strictly for profit. The legal trade in wild cat pelts was once a thriving business throughout the world. During the 1960s the market for pelts grew tremendously as wearing a spotted cat coat became fashionable, especially in the United States and Europe. A typical advertisement from that period demonstrates the mind-set of the era: "Untamed . . . the Snow Leopard, provocatively dangerous. A mankiller. Born free in the wild whiteness of the high Himalayas only to be snared as part of the captivating new fur collection . . . styled and shaped in a one-of-a-kindness to bring out the animal instinct in you."[15]

Such ads sparked tremendous demand, and during the late 1960s, imports of spotted cat pelts into the United States each year included more than 10,000 leopards, along with thousands of cheetahs, jaguars, and ocelots. Coats made from these pelts would often sell for tens of thousands of dollars; the trade in these skins was estimated to be worth nearly $30 million annually. Conservationists, however, were becoming increasingly alarmed that this volume of trade would inflict severe damage on wild cat populations, and in response to these concerns many countries began banning the hunting of big cats.

The most important step in controlling the worldwide trade in wild cat products was a treaty designed to ensure international cooperation in protecting wildlife. This treaty, the Convention on International Trade in Endangered Species, known as CITES, was ratified by ten countries on July 1, 1975. As of January 2002, 154 countries have become parties to the treaty. CITES regulates the trade in wildlife products based on an animal's rarity in the wild. The clouded leopard, snow leopard, and leopard all receive the greatest protection afforded by CITES, being classified under Appendix I. Appendix I species are considered to be at the highest risk of extinction, and in most cases, trade in these species is banned altogether.

Poaching

Although the legal trade in leopard pelts diminished dramatically with the advent of CITES, hunting did not stop entirely. Poachers could still find buyers for the pelts of cats they killed. Poaching for profit continues today, and in some regions has become a serious threat to the survival of wild cats. Even in places where these animals are fully protected by law, buyers can find coats being sold openly in markets. For example, in shops in Kathmandu, Nepal, tourists can purchase coats made from leopards, snow leopards, and clouded leopards. As of 1991, in southeastern China, clouded leopard pelts were the furs most commonly traded on the black market.

With almost no enforcement of wildlife protection laws in some areas, it is little wonder that poaching continues, for hunters can make great sums of money by selling these furs. Eugene Koshkarev, a researcher in the Central Asian country of Kyrgyzstan, explains the poachers' incentive: "In the winter of 1993–4, the value of a snow leopard's skin was more than 60 times higher than the minimum yearly wage in Kyrgyzstan."[16] For the few poachers who may be apprehended, this high reward proves worth the risk of fines or jail time they might face.

During the 1960s, leopard-skin clothing was highly fashionable, creating a cat pelt trade worth $30 million annually.

Poaching is not limited to the quest for furs, however. As awareness of the need to conserve wild cat populations has increased, the market for spotted fur coats has decreased sharply. As a result of this diminishing market, poachers no longer target leopards solely for their fur. They now aim to harvest other parts of their bodies as well. Leopard bones, claws, and teeth are in particular demand as ingredients for traditional Oriental medicine and now sell for much higher prices than pelts. For thousands of years, Asian cultures have used various parts of wild animals in medicines. Though traditionally a minor part of the market for medicinal ingredients, bones from leopards, snow leopards, and clouded leopards are now being increasingly sought. This

Indian policemen display poached leopard and tiger skins they confiscated from illegal traders.

change is the result of the dramatic decline in the availability of tiger bones, which were the long-preferred ingredient. With the number of tigers declining sharply in recent years, poachers are now often turning their attention to other cats such as leopards.

Escalating dangers to India's leopards

The danger to leopards from poaching may be more serious than biologists ever imagined. In January 2000, wildlife officials in India searched a truck and raided a tannery, resulting in the seizure of an enormous amount of leopard and tiger products. According to a report in *Time International*, "The booty from the two hauls added up to a jungle massacre—120 leopard skins, 18,000 leopard claws (extracted from an estimated 1,000 dead cats), a leopard penis, seven tiger skins, 132 tiger claws (from more than 30 cats) and 175 kg [385 lbs.] of leopard, tiger, and other animal bones."[17]

Wildlife officials routinely confiscate animal products from poachers, but the amount seized in this incident stunned even the most experienced conservationists. Manoj Mishra, director of TRAFFIC-India, a conservation group that monitors the wildlife trade, expressed his concern: "This seizure points to the biggest wildlife crime witnessed in the recent past. After all, a thousand leopards killed is enough of a cause for a worldwide concern for protecting the animal."[18] With an estimated Indian leopard population of ten thousand, this crime represents the loss of 10 percent of the country's leopards.

 ## The Trade in Leopard Skins in Ivory Coast

A German biologist, Matthias Gross, in an article he wrote for *CAT News*, made the following observations regarding the trade in leopard skins in the African nation of Ivory Coast.

Many West-African people still believe in their traditional religions. Their life is heavily influenced by nature. Animals and plants play an important role in what they do and believe, and they are used in traditional medicine, voodoo and as symbols of might. . . . Whole skins of leopards *Panthera pardus*, as well as pieces of them, can be found in almost any larger market in the country. Furs or parts of furs of this marvelous cat are sold by fetish traders. The prices range between US $5 and $50 depending on the size of the skin pieces. I found two complete skins, both from very young animals, for $75 each on the largest market in Bouake, Ivory Coast. Leopard furs are also offered to foreigners in luxury hotels and supermarkets. In fact, I was approached in the Intercontinental Hotel in Abidjan and was offered a complete skin for $250. In one of the largest supermarkets, I found two complete adult leopard skins for $130 and $200 respectively.

The local people use leopard skins mainly for traditional medical treatment. They believe that leopard furs are highly effective against skin diseases. Due to this animal's strength and beauty, their pelts are thought to cure nearly every other type of disease too. For a small number of high society people, leopard furs are used as symbols of prosperity and might. I saw some offices of salesmen and lawyers arranged like Natural History Museums. A leopard fur was nearly always featured.

Wildlife Trade in Southeast Asia

TRAFFIC, a program managed jointly by the World Wide Fund for Nature, the IUCN, and The World Conservation Union, monitors and investigates wildlife trade on five continents. A bulletin from TRAFFIC's Southeast Asia office acknowledges that the trade in wildlife products is a serious problem in the region.

Southeast Asia is a major hub of trade in wildlife, functioning as supplier, consumer and an emporium of plants, animals and their derivatives. Nearly all the major taxonomic groups of plants and animals found within this biodiverse area are traded, both within and outside the region, including some of the more important wildlife products in trade . . . timber, reptile skins, plant extracts, and live birds. Southeast Asia is one of the more densely populated regions in the world: Indonesia alone is home to nearly 220 million people. The region comprises some of the world's poorest countries as well as some of the most rapidly developing. In poorer areas, the rich, natural bounty is widely exploited by communities, some just to eke out an existence. In contrast, greater affluence in rapidly developing areas has led to higher purchasing power for wildlife products. As a result of high levels of wildlife consumerism, unsustainable rates of harvesting are threatening species that were once plentiful and bringing many already endangered species ever closer to the brink of extinction.

Until this incident, little attention had been paid to the plight of India's leopards, for conservation efforts were focused on the country's rare lions and tigers. Now, however, there is a growing awareness that the leopard has largely replaced the tiger as the poachers' target. Tiger conservationist Ranjit Talwar estimates that for every one tiger twenty-five leopards are killed. "The leopard is certainly faced with a greater threat. The difference in the numbers of tiger and leopard parts and products seized in the recent past is itself colossal,"[19] he says. Another tiger expert, Valmik Thapar, expresses concern that there are no concentrated conservation efforts for leopards: "What is becoming absolutely certain is that they [leopards] will vanish before the tiger does. The killing game will stop only if there is proper wildlife governance."[20]

Protecting Amur leopards from poaching

Amur leopards, too, have been victims of poaching along the Russian-Chinese border. Because these cats are confined to a relatively small area, however, protection efforts here are proving relatively effective. A coalition of private conservation organizations supports antipoaching patrols in the area. Since the team began patrols in 1998, many weapons, traps, and two leopard skins have been confiscated from poachers. As a result of these patrols, poaching in the area has significantly decreased.

Programs such as these prove that conservation efforts can be successful in safeguarding wild cat populations. With clouded leopard, snow leopard, and leopard populations increasingly at risk as they struggle to survive in proximity to people, significant efforts will be necessary to keep these species alive. Conservationists acknowledge that resolving conflicts between people and leopards and encouraging their coexistence will be the key to these cats' survival.

4

Leopard Research and Conservation

TO ESTABLISH EFFECTIVE programs to protect wild cats, an adequate knowledge base about the species is critical. Understanding facts about a cat's natural history, such as the type of prey it prefers, how much space it needs, or the sort of habitat it requires, is crucial to making sound conservation decisions. In addition, it is important for scientists to have a grasp of the total population of a species in a given area to determine whether that population is in special need of assistance.

Arriving at this knowledge, however, is often extremely challenging. Most wild cats are notoriously difficult animals to observe and study in their natural habitats. They are shy and elusive and often live in environments, such as the tropical rain forest or high mountains, where conducting research can be uncomfortable as well as physically demanding. As a result, the behavior and habits of many species remain largely unstudied, making the planning of conservation efforts on behalf of these cats difficult.

Clouded leopard research

One cat that has challenged researchers is the clouded leopard. The first study of the clouded leopard was conducted by researcher Sean Austin in 1998 and 1999 in Khao Yai National Park in central Thailand. For his study, Austin planned to capture cats and fit them with radio collars that would allow him to follow the animals' move-

Radio collars allow researchers to study leopards' movements from a distance.

ments once they were released, a technique known as radio telemetry.

Austin used box traps, which had been widely used for capturing other wild cat species. When a cat enters the trap, it steps on a foot pedal, which causes the door to shut, containing the cat without harming it. Austin set up numerous traps along animal trails in areas where clouded leopards were known to live, but it was more than fifteen months before a clouded leopard, a female, entered a trap and was captured. Once the cat was captured, Austin injected the animal with an anesthetic to sedate it while it was being examined and fitted for a radio collar. Two months later, a male was trapped as well. After being radio-collared and released, both clouded leopards were tracked by the researcher, who used an antenna and receiver to detect the collars' signals. Using those signals, Austin could determine when the cats were active, how far they traveled, and the size of their home ranges.

Even though Austin gained information on only two individual cats, what he learned provided the first glimpse into the secret life of the clouded leopard. In fact, the radio-collared cats exhibited some behavior that was contrary to what scientists had previously believed. For example, instead of being strictly nocturnal, the clouded leopards were often quite active during the day. The female was active for nearly 45 percent of the observations taking place during daylight hours. Austin discovered that the highest periods of activity for both cats were the hours just before and just after sunset. The animals were least active during the middle of the day and the middle of the night.

Austin also learned that clouded leopards roamed over much larger areas than would be expected for a wild cat of their size. Both the male and female were tracked through ranges of more than twenty square miles, with a core area of thirteen square miles that they inhabited most frequently. He also observed that the cats would travel nearly a quarter of a mile in a twenty-four-hour period. This type of information about the range and movements of clouded leopards will be important for conservationists as they develop a plan for their protection.

Camera trapping

In addition to radio telemetry, Austin applied another research technique commonly used by biologists studying elusive animals such as the clouded leopard—the camera trap. To construct these "traps," researchers set up cameras along established animal trails in the forest. Each camera is

connected to a triggering device that projects a beam of in-
visible infrared light across the trail. When an animal
walks along the trail and interrupts the beam of light, the
camera is triggered to take a photograph.

The camera traps were particularly effective in helping
Austin determine how many clouded leopards were in the
area. Because the cameras were relatively unobtrusive, animals were less likely to avoid the area, as they might have
when a box trap was placed. Because all wild cats have
uniquely marked coats, Austin could differentiate individual animals in the photos and count how many different cats
he saw. In the approximately sixty-two-square-mile region
studied by Austin, camera trap evidence indicated that there
were six or seven individual clouded leopards. Based on
this number, Austin estimated that 100 to 120 clouded leopards lived in the entire Khao Yai National Park.

Although Austin was able to obtain some very important
information about the life and behavior of clouded leopards,

 **Snow Leopard Filming
Breakthrough**

Filmmaker Hugh Miles and cameraman
Mitchell Kelly captured some remarkable
footage during the making of their documentary about the
snow leopards and local people living in Ladakh, India.
Using a video camera rigged with the same type of infrared-
light-beam trigger used in still-photo camera traps, the
team captured the first action close-ups of a snow leopard.
A total of five snow leopards were filmed using this technique. Two of the cats—an adult and an adolescent approximately twenty months of age—were captured on camera
demonstrating behaviors never before filmed. The older cat
displayed scraping behavior, scratching its back feet along
the ground and urinating to deposit scent. The younger cat
showed great curiosity toward the camera, approaching it
so closely in its investigation that it fogged the lens with its
breath. The documentary, including this first-of-its-kind
footage, is scheduled for release in 2003.

his relative lack of success in capturing animals for purposes of tracking illustrates the difficulty of wild cat research in the field. In a report of the results of his research, Austin addressed the difficulty of studying these animals and cautioned against drawing too many conclusions from his findings:

> Before the initial capture there were numerous clouded leopard sightings along roads and seven camera-trap photos. Given the number of trap nights [the sum of the number of traps set on each night of the study] and numerous locations where traps were placed, it is probable that clouded leopards were encountering traps but not entering. At the capture location of the male clouded leopard, a different clouded leopard had been photographed and a live-trap had been open for 15 months. The lack of overall success in this and other studies suggests that there is some inherent behavior that makes clouded leopards wary of enclosure traps and thus difficult to capture for study. It is also likely that, since both cats were individuals with significant previous injuries, they may have been impaired from successfully hunting their normal prey and were behaving atypically when entering the traps.[21]

Despite the difficulties associated with studying clouded leopards in the wild, research continues. In 1998, biologist Lon Grassman began a long-term field study of the carnivores of the Phu Khieo Wildlife Sanctuary in northeastern Thailand. This sanctuary is thought to contain one of the largest populations of clouded leopards in Thailand and is notable for being one of only three protected areas in that country that does not also contain at least one permanent human settlement. The lack of human intrusion, as well as a low number of tigers and leopards that might prey on clouded leopards, is believed to contribute to their high numbers here. Camera trap photographs have revealed the presence of eleven clouded leopards in the study area. Three of these animals were photographed along the same trail within five days of each other. Grassman has captured and radio-collared three healthy adult clouded leopards—one female and two males—and is currently tracking them. The information he acquires as a result of this study will be an important addition to biologists' knowledge of this mysterious cat.

Scientists use camera traps to study clouded leopards in the wild.

Amur leopard research

The techniques used by clouded leopard researchers have also been employed in the study of Amur leopards. In 1993, for the first time, a team of American and Russian wildlife biologists captured, radio-collared, and released an Amur leopard. The goal of the research was to determine whether Amur leopards required large areas of wilderness away from human activities. Howard Quigley and Maurice

Hornocker, of the Hornocker Wildlife Research Institute, an American organization assisting in the Russian fieldwork, expressed the desired outcome of their work: "What we hoped to find instead was that the leopard could move comfortably amid human activity. Except in protected reserves, economic development is already beginning in this part of Russia and is likely to increase. If the collared cat, which we named Svetlana, or Svetta for short, and other leopards roamed freely into these disturbed areas, we could find hope for leopards in this country. We knew that if the leopard could tolerate people, we could campaign to persuade people to tolerate the leopard."[22]

After tracking Svetta and a male captured later for a year and a half, the researchers had reason for optimism. The cats were monitored as they roamed both in and out of protected areas without coming into conflict with their human neighbors. The evidence indicated that perhaps leopards and people might be able to coexist in the region. Quigley and Hornocker relate a story that gave them hope:

> We sat in the field station at Kedrovia Pad [a Russian wildlife reserve] discussing almost three weeks of radio-locations of Svetta in an area north of the reserve. She was within less than 2 kilometers (1.25 mi.) of human activity at times. In the midst of the discussion, a reserve guard named Igor arrived from the north end of Kedrovia Pad. We asked if he'd heard of any recent disturbances in town caused by leopards. No, he said, but about two weeks earlier he had found tracks of a leopard coming from the direction of the reserve. The cat had walked to a logging road, sat and preened for a bit, moved about 100 meters (100 yds.) east on the road and then headed north, straight into human-altered landscapes.[23]

Snow leopard research

Being able to coexist with people in this manner will also prove vital to the survival of the snow leopard. By studying snow leopards' behavior and evaluating their conservation needs, biologists hope to find ways that both people and snow leopards can live together in their rugged mountain environment. Studying snow leopards, however, is extremely challenging. The steep terrain and freezing temperatures of snow leopard habitat make fieldwork difficult and dangerous.

The first scientist to attempt a snow leopard field study was the renowned biologist George Schaller. In Pakistan in 1970, Schaller was able to lure a snow leopard to a bait of goat meat to observe it. While doing so, he took the world's first photographs of a wild snow leopard, which were published in *National Geographic* the following year. Schaller was so taken by his observations of the animal that he conceived a plan to capture and radio-collar the cats. His plan for the first snow leopard telemetry study, however, never materialized. Within four years of his observation of the first snow leopard, seven cats were shot in his proposed study area. The traps Schaller had set to capture his study animals never caught a single cat, and he abandoned his plans.

Other researchers, however, persisted. In 1981, biologist Rodney Jackson proposed an expedition to Nepal to study the snow leopards of the Langu Gorge, a region in the

 Working in the Field

In the article "On the Trail of Russia's Leopards," published in *International Wildlife*, biologist Jack Whitman describes the conditions during the capture of an Amur leopard, demonstrating the sense of humor essential for working in the field.

Female leopard, three or four years old, captured on the night of 23 June. Immobilization completed with blow gun injection. To put it mildly, ambient conditions during handling were a complete nightmare: 1) it was darker than the inside of a cow; 2) the slope was steeper than the west face of the Matterhorn; 3) nobody spoke the same language; 4) gnats left my face a bloody mess; and 5) giant moths accumulated whenever the flashlights were trained on one spot more than three seconds. Ah, the romantic life of [a] wildlife field researcher.

Himalayan Mountains that was home to an abundant snow leopard population. His ambitious proposal to undertake such research was received with skepticism by some who knew that George Schaller had failed at his previous attempt. Nevertheless, Jackson was awarded the prestigious $25,000 Rolex Award for Enterprise for his proposal, and with that vote of confidence, he headed to Nepal to begin his work.

Over the course of the next four years, Jackson and his team captured, collared, and tracked five snow leopards—

Snow leopards are extremely difficult to observe because of the tough terrain and cold temperature of their habitat.

three males and two females. In her account of this research, *Vanishing Tracks*, author and team member Darla Hillard recalls the drama of the first capture, which occurred, amazingly, on the very first night the trap, a wire loop designed to snare the leg of a snow leopard, was set:

> We stopped below the second terrace. Eighty feet above, hidden by the bluff edge, lay the cat. It had seen us coming and hadn't moved a muscle as we approached, melting like a chameleon into the dun and shadow of its surroundings. No wonder the snow leopard is a near-myth. . . . We scrambled over the blufftop and quickly covered the short distance to the trap site. The leopard's eyes, narrow slits of icy green flecked with amber, flashed in the morning sun. Spots of black and smoky gray blotched the dense fur of his off-white body. His thick, yard-long tail whipped the dust stirred by a desperate leap away from the trap and the man drawing near. One huge forepaw, its claws extended, knew the limits of the snare that held him captive. Rod approached quickly. He wanted to get it over with, to frighten the cat, and himself, as little as possible. He stepped up and pushed the stick toward the cat's flank. The leopard flattened himself to the ground, ears laid tight against his head, jaws stretched wide showing two saber teeth, hissing and snarling. Suddenly he lunged sideways as Rod jabbed, deflecting the needle with his free forepaw and spilling the liquid tranquilizer into the dust.[24]

Eventually, the team was able to successfully tranquilize the cat, examine it, and fit it with a radio collar. What they learned from the capture of the cat they called "Ek," the Nepali word for number one, helped subsequent captures proceed more smoothly.

Even though they were living close to their study animals and tracking their locations by radio almost daily, Jackson's team caught glimpses of the collared cats only eighteen times throughout their entire four-year study. They did, however, find plenty of signs of their cats in the form of urine scent marks and scrapes in the earth that the snow leopards made with their back paws. By studying these scent markings, Jackson was able to determine how the snow leopards within the area were communicating with one another—a key question his study was meant to answer.

Studying a Sedated Snow Leopard

In a diary entry from Darla Hillard's book *Vanishing Tracks*, snow leopard researcher Rodney Jackson describes his handling of the second snow leopard he captured and sedated.

> In contrast to "Ek," the immobilization was smoothly undertaken with no significant hitches. I injected a larger dose of drug with the jabstick, and Cat #2, "Dui," was fully sedated in less than eight minutes. She stayed under for nearly thirty minutes.
>
> There was much to do, and Lopsang and I worked quickly. With the tattoo kit retrieved from Customs, we put a #2 in her ear. We also had to check for any wounds; inject Flocillin, a general antibiotic; check temperature and respiration; estimate age based on dentition [teeth]; remove the trap; attach the collar; examine the paws; take photographs; and take measurements.
>
> All her vital signs remained normal, though she had an extended tongue and some salivation, typical side effects of the ketamine [a tranquilizer] and the relatively large drug dose. Her teeth were moderately yellow, with somewhat blunted canines, which helped me to determine her approximate age of two and a half years.

Snow leopard conservation efforts

While Jackson was beginning his groundbreaking research to learn about wild snow leopards, the first efforts to protect them were commencing as well. Founded in 1981, the Seattle, Washington–based International Snow Leopard Trust (ISLT) was the first conservation organization to focus entirely on protecting the snow leopard. ISLT funds a variety of snow leopard research and conservation programs in Mongolia, China, India, Kyrgyzstan, and Pakistan. ISLT programs are designed to work in conjunction with the people living in the communities located within the snow leopards' range. To encourage local people to tolerate the presence of snow leopards, ISLT personnel work to demonstrate the advantages of protecting the cats. Brad Rutherford, ISLT's director, explains: "I think it's an important facet to understand about the trust and how we go about trying to save the cat. That we're not trying to save the cat and forget everybody else—it's working in partnership with the local folks. That's the critical component that sets us apart."[25] One way they have done this is through an innovative program called Irbis Enterprises (*Irbis* is the Mongolian word for snow leopard).

By participating in Irbis Enterprises, families that make a living herding livestock can earn money by making craft products such as mittens and scarves. The items they produce are purchased by Irbis Enterprises and sold directly to tourists, through the Internet, and at zoos worldwide. In exchange for the opportunity to sell their crafts in this manner, the herders pledge to conserve both the snow

Biologist Rodney Jackson was the first scientist to successfully track and research snow leopards.

leopards and their prey. In the two years that Irbis Enterprises has been operating in Mongolia, the program appears to be yielding positive results. Journalist Larry Johnson, who observed the ISLT's program in action during a trip to Mongolia's Gobi Desert, describes the situation: "The first year many of the local women were uncertain that the idea of making crafts would be carried out. They made a few mittens or socks, but not many. When Bayarjargal, the national coordinator of the program returned to the Gobi and paid them for their work, things changed. The following year, the local women made many more handicrafts. Their income doubled from the first year. And in the area studied by the research team, the South Gobi, there were no snow leopards slain."[26]

It was made especially clear to Johnson during a conversation with one of the trip's guides that ISLT's efforts have made a difference:

On the fifth day of the research trip, part of the team headed into the nearby mountains to continue surveys for snow leopards and their prey with a new guide—a local man named

Programs such as Irbis Enterprises have been set up to encourage local people to tolerate the presence of the snow leopard.

Dorj. . . . Dorj, a hunter for most of his life, like Sharov, our
first guide, had killed many animals, including snow leopards. Now, Dorj told us, he thought that the endangered cats,
along with the argali and ibex, should be protected. He said
he wanted his grandchildren to be able to enjoy the wildlife
that he had seen in his lifetime. "I used to have three guns,"
Dorj said. "Now I have three cameras."[27]

The strategy of working directly with local people to preserve wildlife, known as community-based conservation,
has also been embraced by another organization, the Snow
Leopard Conservancy (SLC). This conservation group,
founded by Rodney Jackson and Darla Hillard, conducts
training workshops and education programs for communities in India, Nepal, and Tibet to help local residents dis-
cover ways they can preserve wildlife and improve their
own standard of living at the same time. This type of conservation effort acknowledges that conservation will succeed
only if it is embraced by the communities where it is implemented. Past conservation efforts often failed because the
plans were developed by people living outside the region
who had little understanding of the needs of the local people. Instead of telling people what they should do, members
of the Snow Leopard Conservancy help people make their
own decisions about what they would like to do. In exchange for the planning help they provide, SLC insists that
the groups and people they work with make a strong commitment to participate in and contribute to the program activities. These guidelines are intended to ensure that the
local people have a strong sense of ownership in the projects
and feel a responsibility for continuing them.

SLC has conducted similar workshops in communities
surrounding Hemis National Park in Ladakh, India. During
their meetings with SLC, village leaders were able to discuss their concerns about livestock predation by snow
leopards and develop measures to reduce those losses, improve household incomes in the region, and promote
wildlife conservation. Initially, SLC's efforts focused on
assisting villagers with improving livestock management
and building predator-proof corrals. More recently, however,

their efforts have expanded to help community members find additional sources of income. Because Hemis National Park is becoming an increasingly popular tourist destination, with about five thousand visitors arriving each year, communities in the region hope to reap some of the economic benefits of this activity. SLC has provided the local people with training to develop restaurants and hotels to cater to tourists, and it has given them opportunities to share their unique cultural traditions, such as athletic competitions and festivals. Having an economic stake in the tourists' activities gives the local people a strong incentive to conserve the wildlife that visitors come to see.

In addition to these workshops and planning sessions, SLC sponsors a variety of educational programs designed to teach local people about snow leopards in particular and

The Challenges of Studying Wild Cats

In their book *Wild Cats: Status Survey and Conservation Action Plan*, Kristin Nowell and Peter Jackson discuss some of the challenges of studying wild cats in the field:

Why has science passed by so many of the cat species? In part, it is because cats are relatively difficult to study—they have evolved, in terms of both morphology and behavior, to avoid detection . . . . Cats can be wide-ranging, and this complicates logistics. Cats are nocturnal, while humans are not. Also, even if radio-collared, study subjects are usually rarely, if ever, seen by the researcher. This is not only frustrating, but also potentially limits the data which can be collected. . . .

Outside protected areas, it is necessary to work closely with a number of people who probably understand little of conservation (unlike park research staff), or may even be openly hostile to cats. Where cats are subject to persecution, they can be expected to have developed even greater secretive behaviors, magnifying the usual difficulties of capture and monitoring. Yet it is these cats for which study is of greatest importance. In terms of science, some aspects of behavior (i.e., activity patterns and predation) are likely to differ substantially from those inside protected areas, and understanding these differences is the key to appreciating the scope of species adaptability and evaluating probability of future survival.

conservation issues in general. In Nepal, sixteen villages participated in a snow leopard awareness and education camp. Participants were surveyed both before and after the camp about their knowledge of snow leopards and what is involved in their conservation. Scores of 20 to 40 percent prior to the camp rose to 100 percent after it. In another region of Nepal, SLC sponsors an environmental education program in which instructors in the local schools teach students about the local wildlife and the importance of conservation.

Conservationists from both the International Snow Leopard Trust and the Snow Leopard Conservancy are optimistic that these sorts of grassroots efforts will have lasting benefits for the preservation of the snow leopard and its habitat. Instead of choosing between doing what is best for their families and what is best for wildlife, people living near leopard habitat have a new alternative. After one community meeting, a village elder described his feelings: "This is the first time people have come to talk about protecting wildlife and improving our lives. Now we think we can do both."[28]

5

The Future of
Leopards

ALTHOUGH LEOPARDS HAVE suffered severe population declines because of the reduction of their habitat and persecution by people, conservationists hope that concentrated efforts to bolster their numbers will succeed in ensuring a future for these cats. Efforts currently under way to protect leopards include the development of comprehensive management plans, captive breeding and research programs, and public education efforts. By coordinating their efforts in all of these areas, biologists can address the variety of factors that have caused leopards to become endangered.

Amur leopard management plan

One challenge faced by biologists working to protect the Amur leopard is the lack of awareness of the very existence of this animal. The conservation needs of the Siberian tiger, which shares the leopard's range, are well known, but the leopard teeters on the brink of extinction in almost total obscurity. In a report to the American Zoo and Aquarium Association's Felid Taxon Advisory Group, researcher Dale Miquelle explains his frustration:

> How do you develop both international and local public support for an animal that nobody cares about, or furthermore, that hardly anyone knows about? . . . Despite its perilous status, it has been exceedingly difficult to raise interest in this cat. Most potential sponsors are far away in Europe and America and are unlikely to visit the area or appreciate the

unique status of this northernmost leopard. One noted biologist and cat conservationist remarked, when pressed for support of the Far Eastern leopard, "there are lots of leopards in the world." Of course, he was right, and that is another dilemma for this particular subspecies.[29]

To address this and other problems associated with the preservation of the Amur leopard, a workshop was held in Vladivostok, Russia, in 2001. This workshop, sponsored by the Russian government and international conservation organizations, was attended by seventy leopard biologists from eight countries. It culminated in the creation of a strategy to restore the leopard in Russia, China, and North Korea. Elements of the plan include providing additional protected habitat for leopards, strengthening efforts to safeguard leopards within protected areas, restoring leopard prey populations, and increasing local support for leopard conservation efforts.

Education efforts in the communities inhabited by Amur leopards are an important element of the conservation plan. In this region, conservation traditionally has not been

A man looks at an Amur leopard in a cage. Conservationists find protecting the Amur leopard difficult, since few people are aware of its endangered status.

a high priority for the local people, most of whom do not realize the importance of the unique wildlife in the area. To remedy this, an education center is being built at a local nature reserve in the hopes of teaching people about the conservation needs of the region's wildlife. The center's staff especially hopes to target their educational programs to schoolchildren who will visit on field trips. Other education efforts are conducted by teachers who visit schools to distribute informational booklets about leopards and give presentations about leopards and other wildlife. Conservationists in the region also hold an annual festival featuring activities to raise awareness about conservation issues and to help local people develop positive feelings about nature. Plans are also in place to begin a youth action program in which teenagers will participate in conservation activities such as tree planting, trail building, and leading outings for tourists and schoolchildren.

Amur leopard reintroduction

In addition to these traditional approaches to conservation, biologists have also proposed a more controversial and complex plan—the reintroduction of the Amur leopard. Reintroduction is the process of re-establishing an animal in an area where it once ranged but is now extinct. Since leopard populations existed in other locales in the Russian Far East as recently as thirty years ago, some biologists believe that these populations can be re-created by returning leopards to the same area. Because of the high degree of human development in the region and the lack of wildlife corridors connecting the remaining areas of suitable leopard habitat, there is no chance that leopards could recolonize these areas on their own. The proposed plan calls for releasing leopards that have been born in captivity to form the foundation for a new population.

The creation of a second population of Amur leopards would help to safeguard the subspecies against extinction from a catastrophic event such as a disease epidemic or natural disaster or a decrease in genetic diversity of one of the populations. Implementing such a plan, however, may be impossible. For one thing, large cats have rarely been successfully reintroduced anywhere, since captive-raised cats usually lack appropriate learned skills, such as hunting, that are essential for survival in the wild. The costs of such a program would also be extremely high and would require a long-term investment. Furthermore, the habitat destruction over the last few decades in the area where reintroduction is proposed might make the survival of leopards impossible. In addition, although the reasons for the original extinction of leopard populations in these areas are known, they are poorly understood. Unless the problems they faced in the past are appropriately addressed, any

 ## The Arabian Leopard

The desert mountains of the Middle East are home to another rare subspecies of leopard, the Arabian leopard. Smaller and lighter in color than the African leopard, this cat ranges from southwestern Saudi Arabia and Yemen to southern Oman. It was once considered extinct in the United Arab Emirates; however, recent sightings and the killing of two leopards in 1997 indicate that a very small number still remain. Although scientists have no accurate idea of the existing number of Arabian leopards, one estimate places their population at fewer than one hundred individuals.

The Arabian leopard faces many of the same threats as the other leopard races. Overgrazing of mountain habitat by domestic goats has left much of the area unsuitable for the wild ibex and gazelle that serve as the leopard's food. With the reduction of their natural prey, leopards often turn to hunting livestock, and many are killed by herders in retaliation. Fortunately, the establishment of the Arabian Leopard Trust has led to an increase in awareness about the plight of this critically endangered cat. Through education efforts, conservation training programs, and research into the conservation needs of the Arabian leopard, the trust hopes to preserve this cat in the region. Arabian leopards are now also the focus of a captive breeding program in Dubai, United Arab Emirates.

leopards that are returned will likely succumb to the same factors of habitat loss, inadequate food, and poaching that destroyed the original population.

As daunting as these challenges are, an even greater hurdle to a successful leopard reintroduction program would likely be resistance to the plan by local residents. The return of a large, aggressive carnivore would face opposition by people who are concerned for their own safety and that of their livestock. Any reintroduction program, therefore, would have to work closely with these people to take their concerns into account and determine methods to lessen any negative impact from reintroduction. It may be many years until these challenges can be overcome and reintroduction implemented.

Leopards in zoos

While conservation efforts in the wild places where leopards occur focus on their continued survival, other programs focusing on leopards in captivity are under way in zoos around the world. The management of wild cats in captivity has changed dramatically as the philosophy of zoos changed over the last century. Originally, zoos functioned as living museums with a fundamental mission of entertainment. They were seen as places where visitors could go to satisfy their curiosity about different types of animals. The animals were usually housed in sterile cages without regard for the type of environment in which they would naturally be found. Most modern zoos, however, function as comprehensive conservation centers with a core mission of education and the preservation of animal species and their natural habitat. Animals in these facilities are usually kept in naturalistic displays that provide them with opportunities for behaving much as they would in the wild.

In these facilities, one of the top priorities is the breeding and rearing of species that are threatened or endangered in their native habitats. Although zoo professionals recognize the importance of protecting these species in the wild, they also hope to establish self-sustaining populations of these animals in zoos as a sort of insurance policy

against the chance that the species may eventually disappear from the wild. The success of these captive breeding programs depends on the careful attention given to the genetics of the zoo populations.

In the past, individual animals were bred without consideration for their genetic history. As a result, members of different subspecies or extremely close relatives were sometimes bred, forming hybrid or highly inbred offspring. Hybridizing has been a problem for many wild cat species managed in zoos, including leopards. Many leopards in zoos historically were a mixture of bloodlines from both African and Asian cats. These hybrid animals were undesirable for breeding because they were not pure representatives of any wild race of leopard. Because these zoo populations may someday provide animals for reintroduction programs or may represent the sole surviving members of a species should their counterparts in the wild become extinct, it is imperative that they are as similar as possible to the original strain of animals once living in the wild.

Zoo professionals are attempting to protect various species of leopard by breeding them in captivity.

Scientists at zoos today are able to identify the lineage of an individual leopard through its DNA and records of its parentage. Once researchers determine that an animal has pure bloodlines, it can be added to the pool of potential breeding animals for a conservation program. This type of information is recorded in international studbooks that are maintained for five leopard subspecies (the Amur, Persian, Chinese, Arabian, and Sri Lankan leopards), the clouded leopard, and the snow leopard. Because these studbooks detail the pedigree, or family tree, of each individual leopard in zoos worldwide, they are extremely important for determining how closely related one individual is to another. This information is used when forming breeding pairs; zoo officials make every effort not to breed closely related animals.

Population management plans

Despite the fact that five leopard subspecies are considered to be in need of special conservation assistance through captive breeding programs, there is a limit to the number of individual animals that can be housed at zoos. To give each race the focused attention it needs, groups of zoos in different regions of the world have each concentrated their efforts on a single subspecies. For example, zoos in North America provide space for Amur leopards, zoos in Europe house Persian leopards, French zoos house Sri Lankan leopards, and Middle Eastern zoos house Arabian leopards. (Currently, there are no zoos concentrating on Chinese leopards.)

Within a region, zoos coordinate their efforts on behalf of a particular subspecies. For example, in North America, Amur leopards are managed through a population management plan (PMP), which is a program administered by the American Zoo and Aquarium Association (AZA). The Amur leopard PMP currently manages 76 Amur leopards in North American zoos, but it has identified the need to eventually house up to 150 individuals to maintain a healthy population. The PMP is directed by a population manager, who is responsible for monitoring the genetic health of the group and for providing breeding guidelines for zoos exhibiting the cats. The breeding recommendations provided by the PMP manager are not mandatory, but by participating in the program, zoos can better ensure the long-term success of their captive breeding programs.

Species survival plans

A more comprehensive plan for the management of endangered species in captivity, launched by the AZA in 1981, is also in place in zoos throughout North America. As with a PMP, the goal of a species survival plan (SSP) is to cooperatively manage rare species living at different North American zoos as a single population. SSPs, however, also include strategies for other conservation activities, such as laboratory research, education, and fieldwork. Currently, 145 species are managed under an SSP, including the clouded leopard (123 animals in 34 zoos) and the snow leopard (248 animals in 70 zoos).

A female leopard with cubs. Species survival plans are designed to manage the population of captive-bred leopards.

Each SSP includes a master plan developed by a committee of experts that outlines a management strategy for the captive population to maintain the highest level of genetic diversity possible. The SSP is also designed to maintain the captive population's demographic stability. This means that for the population to be maintained at a certain number, it must consist of a specific proportion of young, middle-aged, and older animals. To arrive at the target levels of genetic diversity and demography, the SSP master plan recommends which individuals should be paired for breeding as well as which individuals should not breed. In some cases, this means that, when necessary, animals are transferred between zoos to create the proper pairings.

In order to maintain genetic diversity within the leopard population, zoo professionals decide which animals are best for breeding.

In addition to overseeing the genetic and demographic health of captive populations, SSPs also serve to assist keepers, veterinarians, and other zoo staff in providing the best possible care for individuals of that species. The SSP management team will often provide zoos with important

information on health care and coordinate research projects to learn more about a species' biological and behavioral needs. The clouded leopard SSP team, for example, produced a husbandry manual that was distributed to all institutions housing clouded leopards. The manual addresses topics such as housing requirements, social behavior, reproductive biology, and veterinary care.

Clouded leopard breeding challenges

In the case of the clouded leopard, breeding information is extremely important, because this cat has proven to be one of the most challenging species to care for and breed in zoos. The primary challenge in clouded leopard husbandry is the difficulty of creating compatible male-female pairs. Often, a prospective breeding pair will demonstrate severe aggression toward each other when introduced; in fact, males have frequently been reported killing the smaller females. Even when individuals in a pair do develop tolerance toward each other, the pair may ultimately experience periods of aggression, ending in injury or even death to the female. In a survey sent to zoos in 1997, eighteen out of twenty-eight respondents reported having female clouded leopards that had been injured or killed by males.

Why clouded leopards demonstrate such aggressive behavior toward one another is unknown. Because so little is known about their behavior in the wild, it is difficult to determine the extent that captivity contributes to these problems. Clouded leopards in zoos do demonstrate a relatively high degree of stress in the face of disturbances or disruptions to their routines. Perhaps, then, simply the stress of encountering a stranger in their environment triggers the aggression.

Fortunately, by comparing experiences in trying to create breeding pairs of clouded leopards, zookeepers seem to have discovered the best way to introduce cats to one another. The key to establishing successful breeding pairs is now thought to be introducing them while they are still juveniles—that is, less than one year old. Many successful breeding facilities introduce cats while they are still very

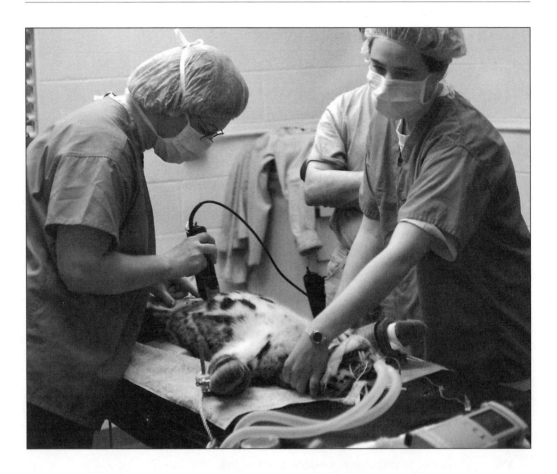

A leopard undergoes artificial insemination, one method of assisted reproduction zoos use when natural breeding is not successful.

young cubs. Most animals introduced at this early age have gone on to form strong pair bonds and eventually reproduce.

Although discovering ways to encourage clouded leopards to form successful pairs and breed naturally is a zoo's top priority, the breeding challenges these cats present has made this species a prime candidate for assisted reproduction. Assisted reproduction refers to a variety of methods scientists use to help an animal become pregnant and bear young. These methods include artificial insemination, in vitro fertilization, and embryo transfer. Artificial insemination is the primary method used with clouded leopards and to date has resulted in the birth of one cub. Researchers are currently studying ways to increase the success of artificial insemination in clouded leopards and are optimistic that improved techniques will lead to more births in the near future.

Zoo education and fund-raising efforts

In addition to focusing on captive breeding of endangered species, the zoos housing leopards are increasingly integrating education efforts into their conservation programs. These efforts include the education of zoo staff, zoo visitors, the general public, and people living in the species' wild habitat. In many cases, zoo education projects are able to link their facilities' conservation efforts with those taking place in the wild. For example, the International Snow Leopard Trust encourages zoos exhibiting snow leopards to participate in its "Natural Partners" program. By donating money to ISLT, the zoos directly support snow leopard conservation efforts in Asia, such as Irbis Enterprises and research projects. The donating zoo can explain this partnership through graphics at its snow leopard exhibit, raising awareness about snow leopard conservation and encouraging the public to participate.

Other, more locally based efforts are under way on behalf of clouded leopards. Concerned that no organization was committed to clouded leopard conservation, the Point Defiance Chapter of the American Association of Zoo Keepers (AAZK) in Tacoma, Washington, began the Clouded Leopard Project, which is a fund-raising and education program centered on the pair of clouded leopards housed at the Point Defiance Zoo and Aquarium. One of these leopards had been bottle-raised and leash-trained after he was rejected by his mother; this animal now serves as a conservation ambassador in the zoo's education programs. Zoo staff members use this cat in presentations that dramatize the need for aiding clouded leopards in the wild. Because this cat draws such a strong response from visitors, the Point Defiance AAZK chapter commissioned artwork of the animal, transferring it to T-shirts and note cards to raise money for clouded leopard research and conservation efforts. The chapter also maintains a website providing detailed information on the clouded leopard's natural history and research that is currently under way. This type of grassroots effort is extremely valuable in raising awareness about clouded leopards, a cat that most people are unfamiliar with.

Incentives to protect wildlife

Although efforts to educate the general public about the plight of the world's leopards are important, the key to ensuring their survival lies with the people who live in areas where these animals are found. Because local people are often the ones responsible for the habitat loss or poaching that is driving leopards ever closer to extinction, they are the ones who must be convinced to protect wildlife and its habitat. Many of these people are driven by poverty and a lack of income opportunities into activities that harm wildlife, so they are likely to embrace conservation efforts that provide economic benefits to them.

One way that communities can benefit from conserving their local wildlife and habitat is through the development of ecotourism, which involves visitors, usually from North America, Europe, and Japan, paying to travel where they

 ### Coins for Cats

Project Survival, an organization dedicated to wild cat conservation, has developed an innovative fund-raising program to support research taking place in the field. The program, called "Coins for Cats," aims to involve students in real-life conservation by having them raise money for specific projects. Participating classes select a field project sponsored by Project Survival and receive a poster that includes details about the project as well as photos of the cats involved. One hundred percent of the money the students raise through car washes, bake sales, and other efforts goes to support researchers in the field. The Coins for Cats program was conceived by Vicky Bloom, a fourth-grade teacher in Reedley, California, who wanted her students to know that they could make a real contribution to wildlife conservation. In three years, Ms. Bloom's class at Alta School raised $1,200 for wild cat research projects, including Lon Grassman's study of clouded leopards and other carnivores in Thailand. Other schools have raised funds for snow leopard conservation and leopard and tiger antipoaching efforts in Russia.

can observe animals in the wild. Ecotourism provides money to local economies by creating jobs for guides, cooks, and lodge workers. Because tourists will only come if they are able to see wildlife, the local communities have a strong incentive to protect wild creatures that they might otherwise see as threats to their livelihood.

A car of ecotourists watches a leopard. The money a community makes from ecotourism gives locals a strong incentive to protect their wildlife.

Not all biologists agree, however, that tourism is a good solution to the problems of many endangered species. In many cases, the presence of tourists has caused the animals to become so habituated to people that they have lost their natural fear of humans and human activity. As a result, in some cases, the wildlife-viewing experience has lost some of its excitement and often feels like a drive through a zoo or theme park. Journalist Matt Murray recounts his experience on a safari in South Africa:

Deep in the African bush, a Land Rover parks daringly, even dangerously, between a mother leopard and her cub. To the right, the mother lounges lazily on her side, her head on the grass, her eyeballs locked on the vehicle. To the left, the cub balances on a tree branch far above the ground, gnawing on a dead impala. The impala's legs dangle down as the cub tears the flesh and skin from the bone—making a sound like the shredding of paper. It would all be a perfectly unspoiled glimpse of nature in the raw were it not for the fact that the animals are actually surrounded by three Land Rovers brimming with tourists and their clicking, whirring cameras. The baby leopard's munching sounds mingle with the squawks of safari guides' walkie-talkies. . . . "The animals are habituated," says Marc Leven-Marcon, publisher of tourism, business and sports magazines in South Africa and frequent visitor to the game parks. "There is an impact on them. They just have to kind of grin and bear it and accept the fact that a Land Rover is going to be there with eight people staring at them." Indeed, as the baby leopard eats his lunch, a fiftyish woman in one of the Land Rovers prattles on about the nature documentaries she has seen back home, and a kid in a Mickey Mouse T-shirt stares ahead sullenly, uninterested in the whole scene.[30]

Not all animals are able to habituate to the presence of humans. As the number of tourists rises, their presence may disturb the very animals they have come to see, increasing stress on the animals and disrupting their natural behavior. Moreover, a large influx of tourists taxes the environment, as described in a bulletin published by the World Wildlife Fund: "Tourists bring their habits and expectations with them. Catering for them in large numbers demands good new roads and hotel complexes. . . . Tourist accommodation can ruin the view, draw heavily on a water supply which may be low at the best of times, and pollute it with sewage. Long convoys of jeeps descend on the game reserves, churning up the tracks, leaving litter."[31]

As an alternative to tourism, some conservationists are proposing an extremely controversial activity—hunting. Though the "big game" hunting of wild cats played a part in their declining numbers in the past, some biologists argue that the resurrection of this practice may in the long run actually help the cause of wild cat conservation. In areas where the leopard and lion populations are large enough to safely allow limited hunting of trophy animals, such as in East or South Africa, this approach might generate revenue for local communities without the environmental problems brought by tourism. Hunters arrive in much smaller numbers than tourists and expect little in the way of environmentally harmful amenities as they pursue their trophies. Furthermore, catering to hunters would not require the substantial investment of building large hotels or purchasing many vehicles.

The change in attitudes about hunting is reflected in a report produced by the IUCN. After years of minimal success enforcing laws that prohibit hunting, there is an emerging "recognition by leaders in many developing countries that their natural biodiversity is a national asset that, if used sustainably, has the potential to contribute to the economic development of their country."[32]

The key to the use of hunting as a conservation tool is in the ability of wildlife managers to accurately evaluate the effect that hunting has on the wildlife populations, and hunting will be sustainable only if it is closely controlled. If managed appropriately, however, both local communities and wildlife populations may benefit. The authors of

Hunters observe a leopard's tracks. Some biologists believe the practice of hunting, if controlled, can help conserve the leopard population by generating revenue for local communities.

IUCN's report explain: "Benefits derived from the management [of wildlife] thus provide the incentive to invest in continued management and conservation of the resource. A positive consequence of this approach has been the reversal in the decline of the conservation status of species and ecosystems that was experienced previously and established wildlife management as a profitable form of land use."[33]

In an essay titled "A Conservationist Argument for Hunting," published in the *Wall Street Journal*, Raymond Bonner describes the financial rewards that hunting can provide to governments that allow it:

> Costa Mlay, the former director of Tanzania's wildlife department, figures that one hunter is worth a hundred nonhunting tourists to his country. Each hunter is required to pay $200 a day to the government—this is in addition to what he pays his professional hunter guide—and there is a 21-day minimum for a hunting safari. The hunter also has to buy a license, and they are expensive—$4,000 for each elephant he plans to shoot, $2,000 for a leopard or lion; $1,300 for a kudu (similar to an antelope). Hunters paid roughly $10,000 each directly to the Tanzanian government during the 1991 hunting season, and the government took in $2.3 million from license fees alone—more than the gate fees tourists paid to enter the country's parks.[34]

Whether it is through the development of ecotourism, controlled hunting, or other programs, governments and conservation organizations must act quickly if they are to keep leopards alive in the wild. In many cases, protecting these cats will take a comprehensive plan to create protected habitat, enforce existing laws, and provide economic opportunities for people in local communities. Some nations appear to be getting the message. For example, the government of India, faced with escalating poaching and habitat loss, recently unveiled a fourteen-year action plan to protect wildlife and improve the standard of living for people near wildlife sanctuaries. After admitting that wildlife conservation has been neglected in their country in recent years, Indian officials plan to take action to care for the wildlife resources of their 89 national parks and 497 sanctuaries.

Why Save the Snow Leopard?

In his appendix to the book *Vanishing Tracks: Four Years Among the Snow Leopards of Nepal*, researcher Rodney Jackson expresses his hopes for the future of the snow leopard.

The skeptic may ask, "Why protect snow leopards?" For one thing, the snow leopard stands as a sensitive indicator or barometer of a healthy mountain environment. Where forage is more productive, so domestic sheep and yaks will weigh more and succumb less to disease. People will have more milk and meat; fewer animals will be lost to snow leopards, which will in turn have blue sheep to prey upon. For another, the snow leopard stands as a vital symbol of Asia's mountains—in scientific jargon, a "charismatic megaspecies." By protecting this species, home for others is assured.

Himalayan mountain fauna are remarkably resilient, and with proper management they can return. Can the same be said for the unique cultures of the people who share the "roof of the world" with the snow leopard? . . . For those of us who have seen the wild snow leopard, there can be no other wish than this: Long may these exquisite creatures roam the cliffs and valleys, and long may they gaze across the wide, untrammeled vistas of their lofty mountain realm.

Only time will tell whether this plan will make a difference in protecting the wildlife heritage of India, a country that leopards, clouded leopards, and snow leopards all call home. Although these cats face enormous challenges throughout their range, conservationists are optimistic that with the support of governments, private organizations, and the public, leopards will always roam the mountains, forests, and grasslands of the world.

Notes

Chapter 1: Meet the Leopards

1. Rodney Jackson and Darla Hillard, "Tracking the Elusive Snow Leopard," *National Geographic*, June 1986, p. 808.

2. Quoted in Darla Hillard, *Vanishing Tracks: Four Years Among the Snow Leopards of Nepal.* New York: Arbor House/William Morrow, 1989, pp. 198–99.

Chapter 2: Habitat Loss

3. Kristin Nowell and Peter Jackson, *Wild Cats: Status Survey and Conservation Action Plan.* Gland, Switzerland: International Union for Conservation of Nature and Natural Resources, 1996, p. 170.

4. Nowell and Jackson, *Wild Cats*, p. 171.

5. Nowell and Jackson, *Wild Cats*, p. 172.

6. Quoted in Environment News Service, "Tiger-Leopard Reserve Set Aside on Chinese-Russian Border," September 7, 2001.

7. Quoted in Environment News Service, "Tiger-Leopard Reserve Set Aside on Chinese-Russian Border."

8. Quoted in Larry Johnson, "Mission to Mongolia," *Seattle Post-Intelligencer*, November 19, 2001, p. A8.

9. Quoted in Johnson, "Mission to Mongolia," p. A8.

Chapter 3: Conflicts Between Leopards and People

10. S.P. Goyal, "A Study on Distribution, Relative Abundance and Food Habits of Leopard (*Panthera pardus*) in Garhwal Himalayas," *Wildlife Institute of India Technical Report*, September 2000, p. 2.

11. Nowell and Jackson, *Wild Cats*, p. 171.

12. Madan K. Oli, "Snow Cats," *Wildlife Conservation*, vol. 96, no. 1, 1993, p. 40.

13. Oli, "Snow Cats," p. 42.

14. Nowell and Jackson, *Wild Cats*, p. 187.

15. Quoted in Nowell and Jackson, *Wild Cats*, p. 220.

16. Quoted in Fiona Sunquist, "Where Cats and Herders Mix," *International Wildlife*, January/February 1997, p. 30.

17. *Time International*, "Stealing Beauty: India's Leopards, Not Its Tigers, May Face the Greatest Threat from Poachers," March 13, 2000, p. 25.

18. Quoted in Devinder Sharma, "New Trend in Wildlife Crime: Poachers Target Indian Leopards," *Environment News Service*, January 28, 2000.

19. Quoted in Sharma, "New Trend in Wildlife Crime."

20. Quoted in *Time International*, "Stealing Beauty," p. 25.

Chapter 4: Leopard Research and Conservation

21. Sean C. Austin and Michael E. Tewes, "Ecology of the Clouded Leopard in Khao Yai National Park, Thailand," *CAT News*, Autumn 1999, p. 17.

22. Howard Quigley and Maurice Hornocker, "On the Trail of Russia's Leopards," *International Wildlife*, May/June 1995, p. 38.

23. Quigley and Hornocker, "On the Trail of Russia's Leopards," p. 38.

24. Hillard, *Vanishing Tracks*, pp. 82–83.

25. Quoted in Johnson, "Mission to Mongolia," p. A9.

26. Johnson, "Mission to Mongolia," p. A9.

27. Johnson, "Mission to Mongolia," p. A9.

28. Quoted in Sunquist, "Where Cats and Herders Mix," p. 33.

Chapter 5: The Future of Leopards

29. Dale Miquelle, "Sharing the Spotlight: Efforts to Conserve the Far Eastern Leopard," *Felid Taxon Advisory Group Action Plan*, American Zoo and Aquarium Association, 1999, pp. 32–33.

30. Matt Murray, "New Safaris: A Walk on the Tame Side," *Wall Street Journal*, December 26, 1997, p. B7.

31. Virginia Campbell, "Elephants in the Balance," *World Wildlife Fund*. www.panda.org.

32. Robert W.G. Jenkins and Stephen R. Edwards, *Sustainable Use of Wild Species: A Guide for Decision Makers.* Gland, Switzerland: IUCN, March 9, 2000, p. 4.

33. Jenkins and Edwards, *Sustainable Use of Wild Species*, p. 12.

34. Raymond Bonner, "A Conservationist Argument for Hunting," *Wall Street Journal*, May 14, 1993, p. A10.

Glossary

carnivore: A mammal adapted primarily for a meat-eating lifestyle.

community-based conservation: The philosophy of including local people in the planning and management of conservation efforts.

ecotourism: The industry that provides environmentally friendly nature-oriented travel.

encroachment: The moving in of people and their activities on wilderness areas.

endangered species: An animal or plant that has been scientifically determined to be at risk of extinction in all or a significant part of its range within the foreseeable future.

extinction: The disappearance of a species of plant or animal.

Felidae: The mammalian family made up of thirty-seven species of cats.

fragmentation: The isolation of small pieces of habitat from a larger whole as a result of habitat destruction.

habitat: An area that provides the physical elements needed by a certain animal or plant species.

inbreeding: The mating of close relatives or individuals with a very similar genetic makeup.

minimum viable population: The population size needed to maintain an appropriate level of genetic diversity for a given period of time.

Neofelis nebulosa: The scientific name for the clouded leopard.

Panthera pardus: The scientific name for the leopard.

Panthera pardus orientalis: The scientific name for the Amur leopard.

poaching: Illegal hunting or removal from private or protected lands.

population: The total number of individuals within a given area.

predation: The hunting and killing of animals for food.

species: A category of biological classification denoting a group of physically similar organisms that breed with each other and produce fertile offspring.

Species Survival Plan: A plan drawn up by the American Zoo and Aquarium Association to help ensure the future of selected species through tightly controlled captive breeding practices.

Uncia uncia: The scientific name for the snow leopard.

Organizations
to Contact

Cat Specialist Group
IUCN/SSC Cat Specialist Group
1172 Bougy, Switzerland
http://lynx.uio.no/catfolk

Part of the World Conservation Union, the Cat Specialist Group is made up of scientists and wildlife experts working on cat research and conservation projects in more than fifty countries. The website provides detailed information on the natural history and status of the thirty-six species of wild cats. Also available through the website is subscription information to *CAT News*, the world's foremost source of current cat conservation information.

Clouded Leopard Project
Point Defiance Zoo and Aquarium
5400 N. Pearl St.
Tacoma, WA 98407
www.cloudedleopard.org

Founded by a group of zookeepers concerned with the plight of these little-known cats, the Clouded Leopard Project works to raise money for research and conservation for both the wild and captive populations of clouded leopards. It also promotes clouded leopard education efforts through the website.

International Snow Leopard Trust
4649 Sunnyside Ave. N., Suite 325
Seattle, WA 98103
(206) 632-2421
www.snowleopard.org

The International Snow Leopard Trust is the world's oldest organization devoted to snow leopard conservation and research. As founders of Irbis Enterprises, this group works to provide people in snow leopard range countries with financial incentives to protect snow leopards.

Snow Leopard Conservancy
236 N. Santa Cruz Ave., Suite 201
Los Gatos, CA 95030
(408) 354-6459
www.snowleopardconservancy.org

The Snow Leopard Conservancy is dedicated to working with local people living in snow leopard range countries, helping them find ways to coexist with this endangered cat. Of special concern is improving livestock management to decrease incidences of predation and improving economic opportunities in the region.

Tigris Foundation
Stichting Tigris
Laagtekadijk 135
1018 ZD Amsterdam
The Netherlands
http://web.inter.nl.net/users/tiger

Founded in 1996, this Dutch organization supports conservation efforts for Amur leopards and Siberian tigers. Projects include compensating farmers for livestock depredation, funding antipoaching patrols, and supporting education efforts.

For Further Reading

Books

Bruce Alderton, *Wild Cats of the World*. London: Blandford, 1998. A good overview of wild cat biology and behavior with individual accounts for each species.

Darla Hillard, *Vanishing Tracks: Four Years Among the Snow Leopards of Nepal*. New York: Arbor House/William Morrow, 1989. A fascinating account of the first study of wild snow leopards. The author describes the difficulties of research in the high Himalayan Mountains and the relationships the team created with the local people.

John Seidensticker and Susan Lumpkin, eds., *Great Cats: Majestic Creatures of the Wild*. Emmaus, PA: Rodale Press, 1991. A comprehensive volume covering wild cat evolution, biology, and behavior, including detailed accounts of leopards and snow leopards. Excellent photographs complement the text.

Periodical

Rodney Jackson and Darla Hillard, "Tracking the Elusive Snow Leopard," *National Geographic*, June 1986.

Websites

Cats: Plan for Perfection (www.nationalgeographic.com/cats). This *National Geographic* site contains an interactive experience for learning about cat biology.

CITES (www.cites.org). This site provides in-depth information on the laws governing international trade in wildlife and wildlife products. Contents include information on

CITES species, member countries, publications, and useful links.

IUCN Cat Specialist Group (http://lynx.uio.no/catfolk). Browse this site for information on wild cat biology and behavior. Also included is information on the status of cats and information on their publication, *CAT News*.

TRAFFIC (www.traffic.org). This site provides detailed information on the efforts under way to monitor wildlife trade. Search the site by region or by wildlife species to obtain up-to-date information.

Works Consulted

Books

Jonathan S. Adams and Thomas O. McShane, *The Myth of Wild Africa*. Berkeley: University of California Press, 1992. An exploration of the history and philosophy of conservation in Africa.

Andrew Kitchener, *The Natural History of the Wild Cats*. Ithaca, NY: Comstock, 1991. An overview of the biology and behavior of wild cats.

Kristin Nowell and Peter Jackson, *Wild Cats: Status Survey and Conservation Action Plan*. Gland, Switzerland: International Union for Conservation of Nature and Natural Resources, 1996. A comprehensive, scientific account of the status of each wild cat species and major issues in cat conservation.

Elizabeth Marshall Thomas, *The Tribe of Tiger*. New York: Simon and Schuster, 1994. A study of the domestic cat in relation to its wild ancestors.

Periodicals and Pamphlets

American Zoo and Aquarium Association, *Felid Taxon Advisory Group Action Plan*, Silver Spring, MD, 1999.

——, *Felid Taxon Advisory Group Action Plan*, Silver Spring, MD, 2000.

——, *Species Survival Plan Fact Sheet*, Silver Spring, MD, September 2000.

Sean C. Austin and Michael E. Tewes, "Ecology of the Clouded Leopard in Khao Yai National Park, Thailand," *CAT News*, Autumn 1999.

BBC News, "India Launches Conservation Mega-Plan," January 21, 2002.

Raymond Bonner, "A Conservationist Argument for Hunting," *Wall Street Journal*, May 14, 1993.

Environment News Service, "Tiger-Leopard Reserve Set Aside on Chinese-Russian Border," September 7, 2001.

S.P. Goyal, "A Study on Distribution, Relative Abundance and Food Habits of Leopard (*Panthera pardus*) in Garhwal Himalayas," *Wildlife Institute of India Technical Report*, September 2000.

Lon I. Grassman Jr., "Ecology and Behavior of the Indochinese Leopard in Kaeng Krachan National Park, Thailand," *Natural History Bulletin of the Siam Society*, vol. 47, 1999.

——, "Ecology and Conservation of the Carnivore Community in a Dry Evergreen Forest in Northeastern Thailand," research proposal, December 4, 1999.

Matthias Gross, "Exploitation of Leopards in Ivory Coast," *CAT News*, Autumn 1998.

C. Hilton-Taylor, compiler, *2000 IUCN Red List of Threatened Species*. Gland, Switzerland: IUCN, 2000.

Michael Hotte, "Compensation for Livestock Kills by Tigers and Leopards in Russia," *Carnivore Damage Prevention News*, July 2001.

——, "Tigris Foundation, Amur Leopard Conservation, Annual Progress Report," October 2001.

Peter Jackson, "China Establishes New Reserve for Tigers and Leopards," *CAT News*, Winter/Spring 2001.

Rodney Jackson, "Snow Leopards, Local People, and Livestock Losses," *CAT News*, Autumn 1999.

Rodney Jackson and Gary Ahlborn, "The Role of Protected Areas in Nepal in Maintaining Viable Populations of Snow Leopards," *International Pedigree Book of Snow Leopards*, vol. 6, 1990.

Rodney Jackson and Rinchen Wangchuk, "Linking Snow Leopard Conservation and People-Wildlife Conflict Resolution: Grassroots Measures to Protect the Endangered Snow Leopard from Herder Retribution," *Endangered Species Update*, July/August 2001.

Robert W.G. Jenkins and Stephen R. Edwards, *Sustainable Use of Wild Species: A Guide for Decision Makers*. Gland, Switzerland: IUCN, March 9, 2000.

Kirk Johnson, "The Clouded Leopard: The 'Littlest' Big Cat," *Endangered Species Update*, March/April 2000.

Larry Johnson, "Mission to Mongolia," *Seattle Post-Intelligencer*, November 19, 2001.

Dale Miquelle, "Sharing the Spotlight: Efforts to Conserve the Far Eastern Leopard," *Felid Taxon Advisory Group Action Plan*, American Zoo and Aquarium Association, 1999.

Matt Murray, "New Safaris: A Walk on the Tame Side," *Wall Street Journal*, December 26, 1997.

Madan K. Oli, "Snow Cats," *Wildlife Conservation*, vol. 96, no. 1, 1993.

Howard Quigley and Maurice Hornocker, "On the Trail of Russia's Leopards," *International Wildlife*, May/June 1995.

George Schaller, "Imperiled Phantom of Asian Peaks," *National Geographic*, November 1971.

Devinder Sharma, "New Trend in Wildlife Crime: Poachers Target Indian Leopards," Environment News Service, January 28, 2000.

Alan H. Shoemaker, "The Status of the Leopard, *Panthera pardus*, in Nature: A Country by Country Analysis," Riverbanks Zoological Park, 1993.

Fiona Sunquist, "Where Cats and Herders Mix," *International Wildlife*, January/February 1997.

Time International, "Stealing Beauty: India's Leopards, Not Its Tigers, May Face the Greatest Threat from Poachers," March 13, 2000.

Xinhua News Agency, "Northeast China Builds 'Joy Land' for Tigers and Leopards," December 13, 2001.

Internet Source

Virginia Campbell, "Elephants in the Balance," *World Wildlife Fund*. www.panda.org

Index

population
  of Amur leopards, 7, 26,
    30–31, 32
  estimating, 8
  of humans, 27
  in India, 55
  minimum viable, 34–35, 76
  of snow leopards, 25, 32, 61
  trends, 25–26
population management plans
  (PMPs), 80–81
prey
  habitat degradation and, 29
  livestock as
    amount of, 46–47
    effects of, 47–48, 51
    reducing, 48–49
  local people and, 31, 32, 33–34
  physical adaptations and, 24
  of snow leopards, 21, 33
  types of, 19
Project Survival, 86

Quigley, Howard, 63–64

radio collars, 58–60, 62, 67
range
  of clouded leopards, 24–25, 60
  cubs and, 16
  described, 15, 17
  of snow leopards, 19, 32–33
Red List of Threatened Species,
  6, 30
research
  on Amur leopards, 63–64, 65
  on clouded leopards, 23, 58–62
  on habitat loss, 29
  obstacles, 62, 65, 67, 72
  on snow leopards, 64–68
  techniques used
    camera trapping, 60–61, 62
    radio telemetry, 58–60, 62, 67

reserves
  in Africa, 36
  for Amur leopards, 35–36
  in Asia
    China, 35–36
    India, 38–39
    number of, 35
  attacks on humans and, 45–46
  costs of, 37
  effectiveness of, 39–40
  establishment of, 36
  management of, 38
  size of, 39
  for snow leopards, 37, 39
  see also specific reserves
Rolex Award for Enterprise, 66
rosettes, 18
Rudyaprayag man eater leopard,
  43
Russia
  Amur leopards in, 30, 32
  conservation in, 75–78
  livestock predation in, 49–50
Rutherford, Brad, 69

sanctuaries. See reserves
Sanjay Gandhi National Park,
  38–39, 43–44
scent, 15
Schaller, George
  on appearance of snow leop-
    ards, 22
  research by, 65
Seidensticker, John
  on adaptations to presence of
    people, 45
  on care of cubs, 16
sight, sense of, 12
size, 18–19, 23
Snow Leopard Conservancy
  (SLC), 71–73
snow leopards

Picture Credits

About the Author

Karen Povey received her bachelor's degree in zoology at the University of California, Davis, and her master's degree in education at the University of Washington. She has spent her career as a conservation educator, working to instill in people of all ages an appreciation for wildlife. Ms. Povey makes her home in Washington, where she manages and presents live animal education programs at Tacoma's Point Defiance Zoo and Aquarium. As the clouded leopard Species Survival Plan education adviser and cofounder of the Clouded Leopard Project, she is strongly committed to wild cat education and conservation.